Southwest

Southwest

John Houghton Allen

Illustrated by Paul Laune

Introduction by Orlan Sawey

A Zia Book

UNIVERSITY OF NEW MEXICO PRESS
Albuquerque

Library of Congress Cataloging in Publication Data

Allen, John Houghton.
  Southwest.

  (A Zia book)
  Reprint of the ed. published by Lippincott,
Philadelphia; with new introd.
  I. Title.
[PZ4.A42664So 1977]   [PS3501.L533]   813'.5'2
ISBN 0-8263-0446-X   77-57532

Copyright © 1952 by John Houghton Allen. All rights reserved. Illustrations copyright © 1952 by Paul Laune. All rights reserved. University of New Mexico Press paperback edition reprinted 1977 by arrangement with J. B. Lippincott Company and John Houghton Allen. Introduction © 1977 by the University of New Mexico Press. Manufactured in the United States of America. Library of Congress Catalog Card Number 76-57532. International Standard Book Number 0-8263-0446-X.

This volume contains the complete text of the first edition, published in 1952 by the J. B. Lippincott Company.

INTRODUCTION

I have frequently stated to my students and still partly believe that the title of John Houghton Allen's *Southwest* is misleading. The book is not, I am glad to say, an interpretation of the great American Southwest; such an interpretation would require more than a single volume. It is, rather, an interpretation of a relatively small portion of the Southwest, the Laredo–Hebbronville–Zapata–Rio Grande City area of the brush lands of South Texas and more specifically of life on and near the Allen Ranch near Randado, in Jim Hogg County.

At a deeper level of perception, *Southwest* is more than a regional study. It is an examination of the idea of Southwest, an influence, a state of mind. Allen may not have been familiar with Henry David Thoreau's essay "Walking," in which he stated that his desultory walks always led to the southwest, where, he wrote, the future lay and where the earth seemed "more unexhausted and richer." Allen's book deals with just such a concept. It is a tribute to a time and a place that exemplified Thoreau's idea of richness; the ninety years intervening between Thoreau's essay and

Allen's book saw the deterioration of the glory of the Southwestern ideal. Thoreau saw the ideal in prospect, Allen in retrospect. Both approved of the dream; Allen was bitter because his Southwest had changed. The more perfect days of his youth were a part of a lost dream.

In an article in *Holiday,* in December 1956, Allen wrote,

> A man can never get away from his home country; it's like running from God. I've been everywhere, done everything, to put Randado out of time and mind. The memories die piecemeal in the heart, but the land returns. It comes back like the image of some woman long beloved and never forgotten. You can take me away from Randado, but you can't take Randado from me.

At the end of the article, after describing Randado and the Jesus Maria Ranch, Allen wrote,

> In the same way I would keep Randado, in the heart. And maybe some day, a better day, we shall all ride back on those little Spanish ponies to Randado, peaceful and cool, to the deep brush and the cool lagunas with the flat clean ground under the whispering huisache trees. It was a land where you had to shake hands with every man, woman and child in the village. Everybody was happy there. It was a land. Maybe we shall all come riding back someday to the little white towns, each to his own Andulucia [*sic*]. All we want back is Yesterday.

These passages give us more than a hint as to the setting, the theme, and the tone of *Southwest,* which was published in 1952. The immediate setting is near Hebbronville, Texas, a ranching area in the brush country between Corpus Christi and Laredo. In Allen's long-lost youth the area was entirely agricultural; when the book was written, it was also oil country. And Allen liked the old days, when things were less complicated, the halcyon days. *Southwest* shows the harshness of the land. It also shows the beauty. The Brush Country is beautiful.

Allen's attitude toward his Southwest was ambivalent, just as was Faulkner's attitude toward his beloved South. Like Wolfe's *Look Homeward, Angel,* Allen's book reveals both a hatred and a love of his native country. Like Wolfe, and unlike Faulkner, he left that country for good and thought the leaving was bad.

Thus the theme of *Southwest* is the glory of a past forever lost. The book is a poetic tribute to "a hard country, brush country, mean country, heartbreak country," which once was "gentler, quieter, not so ugly." He loved the ranches before the coming of oil and prosperity. He was especially fond of the Mexican-American people who worked on them. The tone is both loving and bitter; the basic conflict is in Allen's mixed feelings.

John Houghton Allen was born in Austin, Texas, in 1909. His family owned much land in Texas, including the sixty thousand acres that made up the Jesus Maria Ranch. The short sketch on the book jacket of the first edition states that he attended schools in Texas and Virginia, Texas A&M College, St. Edward's College (Austin), the University of Texas, the University of Mexico, and summer schools at Michigan and Columbia. He also studied art in Paris.

His chief activities on the ranch, the publisher states, were hard living, rodeo riding, and polo playing. He moved to Laguna Beach, California, just after World War II and has lived since in New Orleans and Arizona.

Southwest is Allen's major work, the only book published by a national publisher. He published at least three small volumes before 1952: *Song to Randado* (Dallas: Kaleidograph Press, 1935), a book of poems; *Translations,* privately printed, 1945, a book of French and Spanish poems and essays; and *San Juan,* privately printed, 1945, a sketch which was incorporated into *Southwest* beginning in Chapter 3. In the years immediately following the publication of *Southwest* he wrote for *Holiday* magazine. I have been able to locate three articles in *Holiday:* the one about Randado, mentioned above; an article on polo, the "gentleman's game," in the September 1954 issue; and an illustrated article on Mexico, "the romantic South," in the July 1953 issue. Allen also wrote a bullfight story, "Suicide with Honor," for *True,* ten articles for the *Southwest Review,* and poetry, translations, and articles for the *New Mexico Quarterly.*

Critics have found it difficult to classify *Southwest,* and for good reason. The book is poetic, fictionalized autobiography. It is in places pure fiction. It contains both nostalgic and realistic, concrete descriptions of the land, the people, and the social structures of Allen's Southwest. It is folklore, especially the oral tales of the Mexican vaqueros. It is a blend of fiction, fact, and folklore.

It does not matter, really, which part is fiction. True incidents are fictionalized, and fictional incidents seem true. There was (and is) a Jesus Maria Ranch, but there was no village called San Juan (it was probably Randado). The hard-bitten, polo-playing cavalry unit described in Chapter 7 was based on a unit stationed at Fort Ringgold at Rio Grande City, in neighboring Starr County, on the Rio Grande. Allen's "great-uncle Beverly," who went to Mexico after the Civil War and whose descendants in Yucatan were named Allende, was in reality Sterling Price. Born in 1809, Price led a Missouri regiment in the Mexican War and served as military governor of New Mexico. In the Civil War he was a general in the Confederate army. He died in 1867.

Chapter 1 sets the tone and provides the theme for the entire book. The first fourteen paragraphs describe the village of San Juan as it was after the coming of oil, with noisy, patronizing gringos who would be outcasts elsewhere but who were the "Best People" in Allen's Southwest. They were the loud-mouthed "Typical Texans," who wore "boots with very high heels" and never rode horses and who were "the strong silent men of the West." The Mexicans, he wrote, were no better; both races made him "want to go out and eat grass." Allen believed that the best way to examine the Southwest was "through the bottom of a glass." He was "bitter against the land and these people" because he remembered "when it was a fine place to live." The rest of the chapter sets the contrasting nostalgic tone; in the "old days" things were pure.

Allen realized that his attachment to the old days was romantic. He realized that those times were marred by the *patrón* complex, the White Man's Burden, and the dirt poor condition of the Mexican. Yet he felt that if he himself ever had to be dirt poor, he would rather live among the Mexicans than with the gringos. The Mexicans, he wrote, had "a way of being poor with dignity."

So Allen described all kinds of Mexicans and gringos; the descriptions are of real people. Most of the book is made up tales told by various Mexican friends, fictional and real. A large section relates the narrator's experiences in the border towns on both sides of the Rio Grande; the seamier side of the Southwest is shown.

The last chapter returns to the old Jesus Maria, which was "an idyll, a colonial dream violent and colorful, with bitter things to love." But times had changed. Allen did not like what had happened to his Southwest. The Mexicans had become like gringos, and the gringos had not improved. Allen disliked what he saw.

Whether one agrees or disagrees with Allen's philosophy is not important. And whether things were ever really as idyllic as he remembers them is irrelevant. *Southwest* is well written; sentences, paragraphs, and chapters are finely structured. Both the praise and the condemnation are vigorous; somehow, however, the condemnation seems more vivid. The modern scenes are pictured in clear focus; this is the way things are. The picture of the old days is slightly out of focus, as if Allen realized that romantic nostalgia slightly obscures vision. Bitterness heightened his perceptions, while saccharinity obscured them. And I think he knew that he would never again "ride back on those little Spanish ponies to Randado."

In *The American Cowboy: The Myth and the Reality* (Norman: University of Oklahoma Press, 1955), Joe B. Frantz and Julian Ernest Choate, Jr., pay tribute to *South-*

west, ranking it with the classics of western literature. Discussing early western writers, they say that such writers

> paved the way for such generally faithful novels as Hough's *North of 36* and Dorothy Scarborough's *The Wind* in the 1920's, and for such later fragile prose-poetry as Conrad Richter's *Sea of Grass,* Tom Lea's *The Wonderful Country,* Walter Van Tilburg Clark's *The Oxbow Incident* and *Track of the Cat,* John Steinbeck's *The Red Pony,* Jack Schaefer's *Shane,* and perhaps best of all, John Houghton Allen's *Southwest,* books with an almost filigree delicacy, books that can evoke mood pangs of almost ineffable anguish, books so exquisitely put together that they anger or hurt us more pedestrian writers. (p. 177)

Southwest is, in fact, unique among Southwestern books. It is an evaluation made by a poet, a scholar, of his early environment, which in truth was only a part of his environment. Although he would deny that he wrote as an outsider, he was just that, the son of a wealthy rancher, one who spent long periods at school, away from the ranch, and who eventually left it permanently. His poetic vision provides the chief value of the book, which is a masterpiece of sorts. It stirs the imagination and invites argument as few Southwestern books do.

Orlan Sawey
Texas A&I University
Kingsville, Texas

1

IN THE FIRST PLACE, you have to see this little cantina to believe it. It stands by the side of the dirt road that goes to Zapata, on the Tex-Mex Railway, forty miles from the nearest town in this lost world along the Mexican border. It is forty miles from anywhere, unless you count the walled town that lies behind it, crumbling picturesquely in ruins a half mile away. It is just a little cantina, a place of dubious cheer in a hard country.

For this is hard country, brush country, mean country, heartbreak country. Ugly in summer, drought-stricken, dusty, glaring, but in winter it is hideous. In winter the bare trees, *gran'hena* and mesquite and huisache that the rest of the seasons have a certain grace, these are like a dead orchard. The brush lies all around the ruins of this walled town of San Juan in a graveyard of gloom. The brush is like twisted debris from a hurricane, it is like a bad dream. The nap is up, the whole country seems to have been rubbed the wrong way. The brush lies all around like a dry jungle creeping.

The derricks don't add to the beauty of the landscape. This alone is reason enough for the suicides in the oilfields, it is too rank to look at, and the gringos can't take it. They aren't colonizers, anyway, and this is like a foreign country—you can't blame the poor devils, or their lonely wives. There is not a thing to do in this lonely land but drink and fornicate. The roughnecks say it is worse than Venezuela—it is intolerable, they might as well be exiles in this damned country. You agree with them, you drink beer with them, and beer is a melancholy drink, but there is no whiskey in this hypocritical land, only the bootleg tequila that Margarita serves under the table. They don't even like the smell of it, so they drink the melancholy beer.

They are bilious in this sullen land, with the listless natives looking on without curiosity or intelligence, with the vague air of disappointment, as if they had been waiting a long time, and now they are not bored with anything. The gringos squirm under the implacable stares, but they can't even stare back, because the Mexicans waited a long time to see the gringos, and now the Mexicans are disappointed. So we talk uneasily, self-conscious, of civilization and *white* women and of home with a glint in our eyes, as if this weren't a part of the United States, or some of us just drink morosely while the silent natives stare. It is more elegant to talk, though. The silence can get you down. And there is always that continual eavesdropping, the hollow laughter unuttered.

I know, because I go into the dim dirty cantinas myself, and these suddenly become forlorn places of cheer, I am reluctant to leave these shabby oases in this ragged land,

and I want to stay and get drunk. The first thing you want to do when you hit a cantina in this country is to get drunk. There is something in the air. You are homesick with the roughnecks, and sometimes you can forget the hollowness, you can fend off the cry of desolation, the hunger and gripe that eat at your entrails, you can escape the endless purgatory of the southwest. You are in a country that doesn't belong to the gringo, and that the Mexicans don't seem to want after the gringo is through with it. And better men than you have felt this deadlock, the disintegration, and like going to pieces in this hollow dismal land—in fact, the better they are, the faster they go to seed. The only ones who aren't haywire are the morons, they just get louder.

The flies swarm around your beer, and you brush them out of the foam, but it tastes like the best beer you ever drank. It is hot, but it is rare. And a little peace comes as you warm your belly with the hot suds, and you sit and look outside at the twisted whispering debris of a landscape and you know Venezuela cannot be this bad, you wouldn't mind going to Venezuela.

The best way to see the southwest is through the bottom of a glass. You can take it, after half a dozen beers. You hang around the dim cantinas and actually put off going, lulled by the contagious general inertia and the biliousness; you get a glow and things look better after a peculiar fashion, of a sudden even the dull and degenerate natives seem friendly. You had 'em wrong all the time, they are just shy. You cling to them like long-lost friends, and if you were sober you would give them the back of your hand. You buy them a beer, and they smile, they come to life for an instant in this stagnant land, and forget to look sinister. Even these beggars seem to remember they once were people. They can't help it, if they are stupid. God knows what they are waiting for, but even the buzzards lurk in this country.

There is the damned whispering in the air. You feel you are about to be dry-gulched. Exiled, turned out to pasture, cut off from friends and family and whatever you regard as sweet and civilized. This is a cul-de-sac of a country, you look around and you will have something to write home about—even the rest of Texas looks down on it, and that's saying something. You drink the hot beer in the dark cantina, and when you go out to urinate you are blinded by the sun. You sit there and you get drunk, and suddenly you come face to face with somebody else's conscience hovering in the room. Or a lot of old sins you think you have forgotten begin to eat you alive. Maybe it is the staring, the eavesdropping that stirs the dregs, but whatever it is, you are momentarily looking at yourself in the abstract.

Fingers are pointing, and sometimes the nasty voices say *Dirty! Dirty!* And here you are, a pariah in a land of pariahs. The faces of animals remind you of people you know in the hick towns up the road, particularly the pigs and the bilious chickens, and you tell Margarita to shoo them back in the yard, they look too intelligent. And you'd like to have a woman. It is essentially a fearful land, a libidinous land. You can't turn over in bed in the morning, because you're rutting all the time. It is elementary country, raw and primitive, but at the same time, almost perverted—you live naked with it, and eventually, if you have any intelligence, you will be ridden through this hairy kingdom by the furies. And you know it, you take another beer, so the Jabberwock won't get you.

There is no placating the southwest. Every time you attempt to appease this evil land it tortures you, and it will destroy you sooner or later. It is ingrowing, cancerous, dog-eat-dog, mad and cowardly. Principally it is the damned brush, the dry jungle creeping, heart-rotten, that gets you down. You sit here stewing in your own juice, you put another nickel in the greasy juke box and play Mexican music so loud that you cannot think, and you gulp the warm beer and you spit out the door, or perhaps on the earth floor like the Mexicans. The Mexicans always spit eloquently. And while you are sitting thus, digesting the beer and the background, the panic seizes you. The little *frissons* of alarm crawl all over you like vermin, and suddenly you think, there is no going back. You are never going to get out of this hole. And the panic is so expressive that you get up in a hurry and you find yourself stumbling to your car, stinking drunk, heading for Laredo. You might even end up in a *congale,* if you can do any good. Anything, to kill the loneliness.

The secret to living in this inverted half-world is to learn how not to hate everybody in it, and yourself as well. The people actually spoil the landscape, bad as that is, but you can't blame the gringos because they sour and fester on the Mexican border—somebody told them they had a White Man's Burden to carry, that they ought to be ashamed. But they don't put their best foot forward, and they want to be forgiven everything, because they are Americans. They are usually gross Falstaffian fellows, but without humor, about their melting faces a petulant and perennial cast of grievance. They have black hairy noses sticking out of their pumpkin faces like the beaks of manta-rays. Little noses and little mouths, but Christ! they are loud. They are long-winded and loud, and they don't make the loneliness in this country any easier to bear, and the trouble is, they aren't any better than the Mexicans they despise.

The country is intolerable enough without them, but the rub is—they are your kind of people, mine. Salt of the earth, or they were, before they came to the southwest. This is what the southwest does to your kind of people, mine. Or maybe they can't make a living anywhere else, and here they can be inconspicuous like the weeds and the cacti. Nothing seems to grow in this wasteland but the weeds and the cacti. And the putty faces, the constipated faces, spiteful faces, ruined faces, crybaby faces, mean faces everywhere, scowling in the sun, looking mad all day, dyspeptic—the housewives behind every screen-door like women in cribs—and these faces grow on you, they give you the creeps. These people would live on the wrong side of the track anywhere else, but here they are the Best People.

This is the habitat of the strong silent men of the west. They ride around in new Fords, even though they live in slummy towns and their children have pellagra. They wear boots with very high heels and never ride horses. They walk like fairies, wiggling their bottoms, strangely effeminate, but they think they are fine figures of men. They stand around on street corners with their hands in their pockets, saying hotdamn. They look vastly superior in the pool-hall or barbershop or the Manhattan Café. They clean their fingernails with a penknife, and pick their teeth elegantly with matches, and they talk like hog-callers, they make such a racket that your heart sinks utterly. As if they were afraid of not being heard in this hollow land, or that someone is about to call their bluff.

They've got you, coming and going. Every mother's son is good as you are, understand. If you don't speak to them you are stuck-up, and if you do, you are no better than they are. If they know you they patronize you with a heavy-handed stupid cunning, and they don't consider they have been treated fairly unless you lose money by trading with them. What it is, to be patronized by pariahs! You bend over backwards not to offend their exquisite sensibilities, but it is no use—you get your nose rubbed in the grievance of their inferiorities, anyway. If you mind your own business, they are amateur Texas Rangers. Every cinema in their towns is a horse-opera. At first you think they are crazy, but after a while you begin to look at them as if they were human—you listen to their incredible slander, their venomous drollery, their implacable spite, and you even try to laugh, but you gag first. It is too bad they didn't absorb some of the natural graces of the Mexicans in this bitter land, but to mention such a thing is enough to bring out the vigilantes. Not that the Mexicans today are any better than the gringos—both races make you want to go out and eat grass. The southwest is no place for an amateur to live, but if you live in this country it serves you right.

And I am bitter against the land and these people because I remember when it was a fine place to live. I sit here in dame Margarita's cantina, with the walled town of San Juan enchanted off in the twisted brush, and I discuss these things with the Mexican proprietor of the only store in that almost deserted village—the store was built of boxboards fifty years ago, and it has always been a curiosity in a town built of *caliche* blocks four feet square—and he is a fine old man; he used to be a friend of my father. He is very gracious and dignified, one of the Old Men, a type of Mexican that existed before the wrong kind of gringo came to this land. And there is real twist-tobacco and chili in garlands and *chorizo* in chains hanging from the rafters of his aromatic store, and for sale articles such as tapers and tinder-wicks and Mexican blankets, horsehair bridles, rawhide *riatas,* metates to grind corn, coffee mills and a complete line of the ancient paregorics. And this fantastic old man complains there is no market for such things, nowadays, we have come upon evil times. It was the same kind of stock his father carried, and it is good enough for him, but his customers are different. He shakes his head, and we sit smoking silently for the most part, peacefully during the siesta hour, the old man and I, sleepless ourselves in the glaring day, and I look out from the cool inside of the cantina and I find myself remembering. . . .

This isn't the country I knew as a boy. For a moment I am carried back, and I sit in this old man's store with my father—it was thirty years ago, but we talked to this same old man; he was just as ancient then, just as friendly. It was in a time before men were afraid to be friendly. He made a little ceremony of selling you anything. You were in his house, and he parted with each article almost reluctantly and for very little profit. Almost as if he were afraid of running out of stock, and not having anything to do. We remember those times together, the old Mexican politely and inaccurately, because he is very old, and it doesn't matter, anyway. And I can see through his eyes and my own memory this country as it used to be. This is like the return of the native, but all the nostalgia I feel is for the land I knew as a boy. Before the land had spoiled the people, and the people had spoiled the land.

It used to be gentler, quieter, not so ugly. The villages were built of white-washed *caliche* and thatch and the country was open, without a tree for miles and grass up to a horse's belly. The *mogotes* were confined to the foothills, it was before the brush spread like leprosy over the prairies of this land. The rancheros used to ride the finest horses you ever saw, Spanish ponies, small animals with delicate bones and heads fine as sculpture, Arabians in little. You used to be able to buy them cheaper than cattle from the Viscayas and Benavides, and pretty little mules that were gallant and fast. They were very trim mules, and they were used with bells on their harness, and you could hear them coming in over the road to San Juan. The cattle were Chihuahuas, long-horned, all hide and bone. There were herds of antelope on the prairies. Thirty thousand people lived in what is now the ghost-town of Guerrero—it was before the railway came to Rio Grande—but now all that is left of that great town, that was once as important as Laredo, are a few ornate broken doorways and windows in the stone houses, though the poets say of a moonlit night in Guerrero you can still hear the caravans of Spanish mules clattering down the cobbled street enroute to San Antonio de Bexar.

The old man and I talk of these pleasant things that were, and the Texas-Mexican Railway, that runs between Corpus Christi and Laredo, bankrupt and lame and undefeated, in the red but valiantly holding its charter, this shoves a bedraggled freight train into the weird landscape that stalls a minute at the sentry-box station and takes on water and pushes into the wilderness of brush, its cars empty. There are no cattle for market this time of year, and the oil goes by pipeline. Sometimes there are excursion trains to Corpus Christi, and when the *aguadas* are dry, every summer in fact, the tank cars bring in drinking water to San Juan.

And we talk of other things, of fiestas and more of the elegant Spanish ponies, and the gracious people who used to live in such places as Aguilares and Randado and Zapata, and of one village I remember in particular—that has been razed now to provide surface for the county roads—like a dim dream that has never returned, all whitewashed *caliche* and thatch, that stood by a great lake of water in this arid land, smothered in huisache groves, and that belonged to no land and in no time and which is now gone forever. There was never anything so beautiful as this village in a barren land, you rode out of the brush from the foothills and suddenly you were upon it, and it was so beautiful it made your heart ache, it was like something you had been looking for all of your life. And they sold all the *caliche* buildings to surface the county roads.

You came out of the brush upon it, after a long horseback ride, and you asked why nobody had ever told you of such a place. It was a little walled town like San Juan, and it was built on the drybed of the Baluarte, and it left an echo in the senses, though I can't even remember its name.

2

And I remember, too, the old Jesús María, our own hacienda, our own village, thirty years ago. I drove there with father by buckboard, behind a spanking pair of the little mules, forty miles over rolling coastal plain from the railway at Pena. It wasn't all brush then, only here and there by the dry lagoons or at the foot of the broken mountains were thickets of scraggly mesquite and cactus. In winter it was a land of mist and shadow, of pale shadow and unreal mist, but by summer it would be frying outright in outlandish sun, like the background of one of Remington's paintings. It was a country like Oaxaca and Cordova, places I have been, and San Luis Potosí and Tucson and Santa Fe—that sort of landscape the Spanish seem to carry about with them.

It was strange uneasy country, after Austin, that sad sweet twilight I remember of Austin—it was unkindly perhaps, brutal and raw and humorless, but it was invigorating, it was not as monotonous then. It took from dawn to dark to drive out from Pena in those days, but the country was gracious with golden grass in long valleys when one wearied of the arid wastes and the little mountains. And the spanking little mules went gayly along. And there were three of the walled haciendas to pass, there was a palliation to the landscape in those days. Now there is nothing but brush, and then more brush, the oil-derricks and the ruins, and all the people are sour.

It was just at dark when you were weary and thought you would never get off this endless prairie that you came suddenly, as you did on all those hidden villages, to the old Jesús María. It was one of those lovely villages with belfries and thatched roofs and white walls shining through the green and yellow huisache groves, and at its entrance gate was a squat crumbling fortress like the Alamo. The village was surrounded with the fern-like huisaches, their blossoms like gold pieces and fragrant with a heavy scent. All the old haciendas stood on these moat-lakes smothered in the lovely huisache groves.

There was a rare peace about these villages. Every one of them was a toy of a hacienda lost on the verge of Nowhere, they were built by rude violent men in a golden age when these people belonged to neither Texas nor Mexico. They lived between the Nueces and the Rio Grande in a sort of colonial past, and even their language was rich and phonetic and antique. This was the land on the old maps that was marked Wild Horse Country. Very little was known about it, and the people in this lost world never wanted it changed, but it was changed, for all things change. They had built their white roads gleaming, and every day of their lives they longed for peace, even as the good padres do; but they had not time for it—they lived violently, as all men must, until the evil days came on them and they lived not well. And then all that was left for them was to remember the peace they never had, and the white villages, and the huisache groves on the moat-lakes.

I can remember those villages well. Horses were tied in front of the *jacales,* in the tattered huisache shade, standing placidly. Herds of goats, the leaders belled, wandered tinkling down the cobbled streets. And in over the white *caliche* roads the children came driving milkcows. They were always laughing, the brightest and most whimsical children you ever saw. And they came to the store to look in at the gringo child, or to smell the black twist-tobacco and saddle leather, and gaze at the candy in the jars like little heathens. Their fathers in large felt sombreros, rawhide leggin's, with enormous spurs jingling—seemed always to be driving herds of horses into the mesquite corrals— duns and *grullos* and bays with black points and sorrels like red-headed laughing girls and tiny grays fine as silver. These thundered into the water and were loath to be penned, creating a splash and fury, kicking and whinnying and cavorting and some of them galloping free to their long valleys again. Spanish ponies, hundreds of them, until every hacienda looked like a horse-ranch.

I had my own horse, and I considered myself a *jinete* when I was seven years old. At eight I was herding cattle with the vaqueros, eating the execrable and indigestible food in cowcamps, sleeping on the trail with my saddle for a pillow. And then, when I was nine, I was riding ungovernable horses, alas. They were invariably too much for me, but I could not resist the rare temptation to ride these

Spanish ponies. Spanish ponies, grown horses in miniature, lovely to look at, larger than Shetlands, and about as treacherous. They had hard mouths, and heads like burros. And the day came when one of these little horses took the bit in its teeth and ran through the lagoon brush with a terrified burden on its back, and I was the burden. It probably served me right.

The branches beat me in the face and stifled my screams. The horse went crazy and bolted into trees and fell back stunned, then lunged ahead like a stallion on a line. It was just an oversized Spanish pony, but it had a mouth like a race horse, a manic disposition, and I was helpless on its back. I didn't have the sense to jump off—I was too busy trying to holler. I must have looked a scarecrow rocking back and forth on that insane animal. I never did know what caused it to act like that, it bolted out of the blue, and I hadn't done a thing. But perhaps being Spanish, it had the *coraje,* it was bored with life. Even the horses have *coraje* in the southwest.

It was a marvel I survived this experience, for the vaqueros at first had been unable to catch my bronc on the jaded animals they were riding at the end of the day. Finally, they ran it down in relays, shortening their circle on the runaway as they do when chasing mustangs, until a clown of a Mexican named Javier, who had never had a serious moment in his life but for once was thoroughly frightened, took me shuddering from my spent horse onto the saddle with himself—soothing me urgently, for there was a great deal of blood. It ran on the lathered shoulder of the horse, I remember, and it stained Javier's jacket. There was not a shred of clothing on my back, and my leather chaps were in tatters. My face and chest and skinny arms looked like

I had run a gantlet of bullwhips, but I was crying most because my chaps were ruined. The men who had taken part in my rescue were torn and bruised, their horses desperately lamed. As for the one I had ridden—a beautiful little dun animal, almost like a fawn, lovely to look at—it ran a few hundred yards further and stood for a moment surprised, then dropped dead in its tracks. None of it made sense.

"Por Dios!" I remember Javier saying white-faced to my mother, and for a rough man he could be very tender, "it was a stubborn beast. And I had fear, madonna, I was afraid." After that, I was like a Chinese that Javier had fished out of the river, he practically had to adopt me. And since I wanted to be a horse-tamer, it was Javier who taught me several years later to ride the rough ones, the improved breed of horses we called Billys. When I was thirteen, Javier taught me all about mean horses. Javier could ride anything with hair on it, and he had me riding wild mares that bucked so hard I got off of them spitting up blood. It takes a heavy unbroken mare to really buck. I was seldom thrown, because Javier taught me balance, and there was a lot more barrel to the Billys, they even bucked more honestly than Spanish ponies. You feel like you are riding a rail when a Spanish pony starts to buck, you can't grab with your knees or spurs anywhere.

Javier would catch up one of the Billy mares in the mesquite corrals, snub it to a post, saddle it with one hand while the thousand pounds of affronted femininity kicked out in four directions, give me a neckrein and a push up, and turn the animal loose without a bridle. Those mares tried to turn inside out. They had never had a rope on them before, and they went sunfishing and squealing as if I were gaffing them with the spurs, which of course, I was—but only to stay on. I had to stay on any way I could without clawing leather, because Javier would not approve of that, and Javier was my friend.

They skinned out of the saddle sometimes jumping backwards, and they fell backwards if I rode them with a snaffle in their mouths. You'd think they had barb-wire in their mouths, if you rode them with even a snaffle. They somersaulted sometimes, just about the time I was getting the hang of riding them with my knees, and I can tell you it was difficult when you are straining to hold them between your knees, to get thrown clear. Your reflexes aren't that plastic, that's where the best rider fails. It was all rough stuff, but I liked it, or I thought I did at the time.

I have always remembered riding horses with Javier in the brush corrals. The brush corrals were what I was afraid of most, of the mares bucking along and my chaps catching on a post or a snag, and of being quartered and drawn. I came out of it though, without even a broken leg—and when I got pretty good, Javier let me ride these broncs in the open.

It was all a little too raw, and the violence was always too much. It was a savage land, a Tartar's land. When I was eight years old, I saw a vaquero gored by one of the Chihuahua bulls, stuck to the ground, literally. But he rode to camp supporting himself on the swell-fork, and I remember how straight he rode, like a cavalryman—and how he died screaming and not at all bravely the next day. That was the way with them, Javier said, the vaqueros always died like coyotes. And I can remember the long droughts—the blear-eyed herdsmen in clouds of dust, holding back the starving cattle, I can still hear the noise of the pear-burners, like an inferno.

And I remember the brutal goatherders, at whom even the vaqueros looked askance—miserable, whimsical wretches who had been small banditti and came out of Mexico because they didn't want to be shot and worked for practically nothing and whom all the ranch children adored—full of wonder and ignorance and bloodshed as these men were, showing their machete-scars from the revolutions and spitting on the ground with venom when they talked of Carranza, but they could be gentle with a child, and they played sweet plaintive music on rude-fashioned reeds. When these *pastores* looked at a child, they made a little prayer, and they put their dirty hands on its head, so as to be sure not to give it the Evil Eye.

I have often wondered if my instability, my immoderation, even the damned ennui came from this conditioning I received as a boy on the Jesús María. Perhaps I was too sensitive to the brutality of this raw violent land, and it has made the rest of my life seem like an anticlimax. Something left its mark on me. Maybe it was riding the wild horses with Javier in the brush corrals, or maybe it was working in the cowcamps, roping the Chihuahua cattle that hit the end of your lariat so hard they often jerked your pony down—something was wrong. It was all a fine raw time, in its proper place, but I guess I had been too young. And of course, it was mad, that whole country was splendid and mad.

I remember grubbing out *senderos* with the Mexicans until my hands bled, and thirsting on tedious cattle drives until I slapped the cattle away fom the water trough and drank myself stupid. Ever since I can remember I have had that intolerable thirst, eating me alive. And branding in the hot August sun was a thirsty job, mugging down the calves with my finger in their slobbering mouths, and holding them by a leg and tail, a knee in their belly while they were castrated and branded. Branding was done during the still smothering dog-days because of the screw-worms —even the flies went away in August. Some of those calves you wrestled weighed four hundred pounds, you felt you were breaking their necks to mug them down.

Christ, it was hot in those mesquite corrals, they were more like barricades. No air came through and the dust went straight up and hung over us like a canvas. You drank the bad water in the *jolla* under the chute and there was no shade, and your hands trembled and the water ran out the spout and down your grimy shirt. You put in a rest by the branding-fire, and ate the mountain-oysters that were broiling on the coals—they tasted a little like egg, and the cord part like clams, and they were supposed to put lead in your pencil. The Mexicans would eat them and laugh, and hold up their bare arms, pulling back a sleeve, for all to admire.

You dug postholes by the mile, you were always fixing the everlasting windmills that were aggravating and unpredictable as outboard motors, and you hated the windmill work worst of all. Sundays you cleaned up and took a half-day off, and played monte in the bunkhouse and usually lost, easy come, easy go. But what left its impression forever was driving the damned cattle to the Tex-Mex Railway forty miles from the Jesús María, seven or eight times a year—the monotony, the dread tedium of it got me down, it was something I hated like hell. I guess between the time I was twelve and fourteen I must have been on twenty cattle drives, and they always got me down. They were something I never got over, perhaps. I haven't any patience now—the very use of the word tedium makes me mad. I was burnt out of my ability to stand tedium by the time I was fifteen.

It was not so bad when we were driving at night, when the cattle moved along, and it was cool. There were clouds of stars in the sky. The vaqueros sang *Ay, ay de ay* or *Allá en el rancho grande,* or stanzas of the whip-spur '*Cucaracha,*' the rollicking '*Cucaracha*' because they could remember the raids by Pancho Villa. And Guiterrez used to talk of the old times, of priests and hidalgos cruel as blades and proud as Satan, violence and contrast almost beyond belief in our day, and color that died in this land a long while ago. There was the tale he used to tell under the stars, as the herd moved along, of Don Sebastián who murdered his wife because another man desired her, and castrated his only son in a rage. He was a monster, Guiterrez used to say, but somehow you couldn't get away from the fact that he was a man. There were men in those days. She was innocent, a good woman—and why did he kill her, señores? Why, because he loved her, it was that simple. The boy still hung around the cantinas, weighing two hundred and fifty pounds, with a voice like a sparrow, we all knew him.

In the heat of the day, though, it was deadly driving cattle. They shuffled along with their tongues hanging out, and you couldn't move the herd any faster than the slowest cow and calf. This was especially true of the Herefords, that we hated. The heat sweltered down in the dust or it shimmered in mirages before your eyes, and you tried to spit but your throat was dry, and little calves lay down besides the trail to die with their tongues hanging out a foot. The buzzards were after their eyes and tongues the first thing.

I hated those sluggish Herefords and all the vaqueros hated them, we used to cuss the old man for having introduced them into the country—they gave us the *coraje,* that blind unreasoning hard-headed rage the Mexicans have, over trifles usually, because it is really nothing but a revolt from the terrific ennui. Or it can be that sick rage that seized Don Sebastián when someone defiled the woman he loved by just looking, and he killed her like Othello. I've had it off and on throughout the years, so violently that it has made me sick, and usually about trifles. It has been an intolerable burden for a gringo, and it has left me frustrated and dishonored and unexplained more than a number of times, for it is hard to have a head like a gringo and the heart of the Mexican. But what would you, in the *coraje,* in the battle between your emotions and your common sense, it is always yourself you are afraid of. . . .

The Chihuahuas were not so bad. They moved along at a trot with their huge horns shaking, a little like elk. And they were never so tired that they did not stack up like a deck of cards against a fence when even a wagon passed, as if they had never seen one before, and if they did not knock the fence flat they jumped it beautifully, the whole herd of them, and we had a diversion, roping and riding, to get them back. It was like driving wild horses, but most of our driving was the butterball Herefords and not so exciting—they lolled along with their tongues hanging out, and they gave us the *coraje.*

We tried to ignore the monotony, and we walked our horses at the pace of Beethoven's Death March, roping despondently at the feet of the cattle and wishing they were dead, or dreaming perhaps of the next rodeo, or more than likely, just the next waterhole, where we could get a drink of muddy water after the cattle got through with it. You could always ride out to the depth of your horse's belly and scoop up a little palatable water in your Stetson. I tell you, the thirst we suffered was intolerable. You didn't carry water, that was sissy stuff, and besides the canteens were lost in the brush. So you lived for the thirst and by the thirst, Jesus—it was all you could think about! And you swore when you got to town you would drink a tankful of beer. You never got enough to drink, you were either starving for water, or logged down with it like a barrel and unsatisfied. And with this thirst it was the last straw to have to wait along behind a herd of butterballs, it was boredom, monotony, tedium enough to make you scream. It reminded me of the Retreat from Moscow, but that just goes to show you how my mind works. I used to try to think of something diverting on these long drives, but I was too disgusted, it was too hot and dusty, I was too tired and thirsty.

The dust washed down my face and into my grimy shirt with the sweat, I was sticky with filth, caked with dust, I couldn't even breathe through a bandana. I used to dream of long cool lemonades, full of ice—and at least that was a good thing, for if ever I got a cool drink, I had the thirst. The devil himself could have come along and I would have sold my soul for a drink of cool water. And then sometimes when I got to Pena, all that it made me was sick. But I used to dream of the long cool drinks just the same, I was dehydrated, and I was willing to ride five miles out of my way for a good drink of cool sweet water.

I used to dream of sparkling grapejuice with a shot of tequila in it for a kick, full of ice, full of ice. The only reason you went through with any of this was to get a drink of iced water. Yes, it was the thirst of torture, and it was fatigue like a drug, boredom like death, and sometimes we lived in this purgatory for twenty hours without relief. The boredom crawled on you, it ate you alive, and if you were anything but a moron, it marked you for life. You try to swallow, but you can't, and you think unless you have a drink of water, you will go crazy. Your mind begins to wander. The heat waves roll in the oily air. And you see that mirage again, the glittering city, waving, shimmering, elusive, marvelous as rain, and it looks like Paradise. But you would go to hell for a drink of water. You would give ten years of your life for a drink of cool water. And the *coraje* comes over you, and you damn the Herefords, and the monstrous vaqueros, and the god-damned country and everybody who is stupid enough to live here. The bile comes up in your gorge, and there before your eyes, all shattered in the dust, lies the City of God. There was something about those drives that I never got over.

It was hard country, even then, I remember. I turn to the old man sitting with me in the cantina, and I say it was a hard country to love, and then only bitterly, as men love bitter things. And I light a cigarette and I say to the old man, to hell with it.

3

B UT I CAN'T dismiss it that easily—it fastened on me, like Catholicism, when I was young, and every time I've tried to get it out of my system I've felt like an apostate. And it did have its side, a certain epic quality. It might never have been as extravagant or curious, but I wanted to believe there were giants in those days. And these are a poet's tales, a young man's tales; they were my first loves. I have felt about these stories as I still feel about the first time I visited Monterrey, when it was a fair colonial town, and not the bordello, the Naples of Mexico as it is now—but my first foreign city, when I was young, and everything passing strange.

I got there somehow by train from Laredo—it was more than twenty years ago—arriving in Monterrey when one arrives at all Latin American destinations, unaccountably, in the early hours of morning. And clattering down the cobbled streets in a dilapidated hack, the driver urging his skinny steed practically with whip and spur, ringing a cowbell like mad at every deserted corner where the drab lamp shadows fell, making enough noise to wake the dead but never the good people asleep in that town, it was comic and it was ominous and it was grand, my first exhilarating experience in a real foreign city.

Certainly I felt like a person of consequence, flying past a whole dark town shuttered at every window and door, as if the lodgers were expecting another raid from Pancho Villa and his Dorados, breaking a silence so thick that it closed after us. There was a suppressed excitement in this terrible silence, as if the householders would suddenly come awake and violently—the smell of their ribald revolutions was in the damp air like an ambush. The *cochero* beat on the door of a hostelry, accepted a peso in great haste and clattered off, leaving me to be ushered into a patio that was cool and still except for the song of birds, and dark behind the candle in the padrone's hand but for the white oleanders glowing by every archway. I have never forgotten those oleanders, or the fragrance of that particular patio—a giant bougainvillaea grew up the side of the stairs. The stairs were almost stately in the luminous dark. The mockingbirds were singing actual arias from light opera, snatches of the *'Golondrina'* or the *'Cucaracha'*—so distinctly that I almost heard the hoof-beats in the *'Cucaracha.'* What a Never-Never dark that was, and how I remember that patio with something like pity!

Monterrey was my first foreign town, this was my first trip into the interior of Mexico. And I suppose it cannot be truthfully said that I was never young. I was young that once, at least. Even in the darkness that morning I knew that I would love Monterrey; I had imagined beautiful parks and statuary, fountains playing in Moorish patios, rare spiced food fit for gourmets and golden Manzanilla, beautiful señoritas with lace mantillas to their hair—ah, it was better than I ever expected or deserved, a thousand times! Oh rare first thrill, Oh raw young man—I was in the clutch of a strange excitement I was never to feel but this once, because you feel it once, and never again. I waited there in the early dawn, alone, sitting on the foot of my bed, open-mouthed with expectation, for a fierce beauty, for a rich wondrous unreality that would unveil itself at sunrise.

What else had I expected? Dim tropical lands, perhaps, and fountains of gold, and luminous rains with gargoyles flying on lost cathedrals, and splendid horses caparisoned for princes stepping through the cobbled alleys of misty cities, and ships standing out from walled towns in sunless seas—that was the gist of it! But there was something more, it had seethed through my veins, screaming Freedom and Youth! Youth! Youth! A farewell to peace, the devil-may-care, and I don't know what else. I had been ready for anything at that moment! And no matter what that brief pathetic spell was, I have remembered it, and nobody can take it away from me—and though the break of day showed me nothing but a little city of flat-topped houses and dirty streets and bare plazas and poor beggars and black peon women, I have never forgotten my first impression of Monterrey in the early hours, before the enchantment died, or the patio in the darkness where the white oleanders grew and the mockingbirds sang.

And in the same way I have remembered the Old Men, and I have come back to the dim dirty cantinas to listen to the high brave words of such as Ernesto Acuña, who is the very last one of Don Juan's vaqueros. He is a very old man, his eyes are dim and watery and his face is wrinkled like a hide in the sun. The limed rafters and the once-white adobe walls of dame Margarita's cantina are a dirty yellow, there is a stench about the damped earth floor, and what the Mexicans call *animales* are in the thatched roof. The fat wench brings mescal and tequila which have the flavor of wild pepper, and Ernesto and I talk until the cows come up. He nods and drones, his old body creaking like a chair when he moves, his tattered felt hat shading his furrowed cheek and his bristling eyebrows from the candlelight—of haciendas, of the old dons and their mistresses, of broad acres and the white roads gleaming, of priests and minstrels and good horses, with a strange streak of tenderness in such a fierce old man, but Ernesto was never ashamed of sentiment. He was a man, and he had lived in a time when you were only half a man, without sentiment.

"You believe in a man by the spurs he wears," Ernesto asked me, "or the horse he rides? Then I will tell you of Felipe.

"He came riding out of the brush from Zapata way—it was thirty years ago—on a log-headed brute much scarred by the chaparral. He was a rigid little man, gnarled and bowed and wiry, and a cross-eyed *mozo* rode behind him like an esquire. There was a touch of the manner about Felipe, he might have been some petty hidalgo, and I shall tell you about the idiot Lili, also. Lili wore fresh hide leggin's over cloud-white pantaloons, and the large rowels of his cheap spurs jingled like castanets. He breathed hard, he jerked at his iron curb, or he rested his palms—an elegant gesture —on the huge pommel of his *charro* saddle.

"Felipe was practically afoot, accompanied by this clown, he didn't look the part, but he was a vaquero, señor. One of the best. His eyes were bloodshot from the dust. He was lean and fierce and pig-headed, the kind that is kept in the rain and under the stars the year round, paid four bits a day to break his bones and kill good horses, and discarded like an old saddle blanket when his service is done. He worked in the brush, in country you can't get a *white* man into, and men like him rot in thickets sometimes where they fall.

"Felipe was brave as a lobo. He was no more afraid of spoilt horses or somersaults through the brush than frijole or tortillas—a *valiente* he was, a man of blood, passionate and faithful and unforgiving. But we laughed at him; he was ridiculous. He had probably never in his life been laughed at in the dark country he came from, but we could not help it—had he earmarked us each time, we would have laughed.

"He was skilled with the lasso, like all *charros,* but left-handed and awkward as a woman throwing rocks. He could rope wild boar and antelope, give him the horse to do it on, and in the corral he could forefoot anything, anyway. He adopted our own conceit of roping *all* cattle with the lariat tied fast to the saddle horn. Other vaqueros rope and wrap on, dally it's called, but we in our pride and skill at the San Juan lived with our lassos tied to the horn and our saddles cinched to broncs. It was the honorable thing, you see, it was what gave us a name—it was the San Juan!

"A steer splitting about on the end of your rope, in the heavy-branched thickets, the horse snorting and jumping or bucking outright, the vaquero flipping his lasso on this side and that not to become entangled, forking and yanking his goddamn bronc, dodging brush and high cactus, protecting himself and his fractious mount from the charges of the steer or its weight as the rope went taut—there was no way in all the world to let go or back down from the job in front of you. Felipe liked that, there was salt in it. He liked being yanked about, he liked the shock and the rage. He had more falls than any of us, but he would land in his droll positions or be so shaken with fury that we would laugh. The *coraje,* señor, he had the *coraje.*

"He did not deserve all our laughter, nor did he have a fall every day. He was a great one to celebrate in the village and, when he treated, he had friends. I have seen him laugh and slap his thigh and almost swallow the cigarette that seemed always to be stuck to his lower lip—and drink! the man had a hollow leg, drinking as much as three bottles of tequila at a sitting. Of that which he has done, he was remembered most for this, and it is always said, that Felipe had a hollow leg. We laugh to think of him. He was tough as a boot, but he had his side, as Javier used to say, though the thought of him made us laugh out loud at supper, while he and Lili would sit away, feigning not to hear, smoking shuck cigarettes in the dark.

"You would have mocked him, too—flushing their cattle from *mogotes* or downing a steer between them, Felipe and Lili. Lili spurring furiously and getting nowhere, beating his nag around and about, casting endless and wasted throws at the hind legs of the animal, fuming in the dust, all arms and rawhide chaps and lariat, a lariat forty feet long that he used like a travesty on the work of any vaquero born. He would stand off finally—crestfallen; his rope knotted into innumerable tangles, his potbelly bulging out toward the bowed and despondent neck of his mare, for this clown rode mares, his little fat face fixed with awe, self-deprecation and the most painful grimaces, looking as if it hurt him, he was that ugly."

Oho! and I listen to the rich raw words, I marvel at the expression that the illiterate can have, and I feel like cheering—this is something, this is no idyll of the Californias, no be-sashed, singing and laughing vaqueros with long flapping toe-fenders to their stirrups or silver-mounted harness or jackets embroidered, but this is a tale of the violent and untamed, of the Old Times, told by the last of the Old Men as he spits on the dirt floor and drinks tequila—with a lick of salt and lemon to make it flavory—in the background the ruins of the walled town of San Juan, which was his *patria,* his own country. And I listen, homeless myself, as the old man speaks his part, in Spanish phonetic and antique that I seem instinctively and with sympathy to understand.

"August was the hardest work of the year," he said. "We had to comb the Little Mountains, a short range of gravel hills no higher than three or four hundred feet but covered with pear and thicket so densely that machetes were used as much as lariats, you had to cut your way through that dry jungle. We had the whole area laned with *senderos* and right-of-ways, or we would never have been able to get into it. The worst of the ladinos lived in this country, and sometimes we were there a couple of months before we drove a good catch out to the basin that lay on the other side and that goes down to the valleys of San Juan.

"Kill thy horse, kill thyself, but rope and hang on. Those were the words in the other days, señor. We ran them down to traps and into snares; we ran them into bluffs, and like wild horses, into the corners of canyons—cattle that had never been branded, wild-eyed, sabre-horned, fleet and vicious as wild boar. And like wild boar they lived in impenetrable thickets, eating the thorny cactus for their water and never approaching a reservoir. And like the wild boar they moved in the thick shadows of the brush, covered from the light of the sun and half-blinded by it when you jumped them into a *sendero*. They were the ladinos, some of them nine and ten years old before we ever caught or branded or sold them. And some of them we never caught, they were wild as deer, and we hunted them down with rifles.

"We combed the brush, we went tracking and hounding and halloing after a glimpse of them in the heavy shadows. It was so hot and still that you would sweat up your jacket like a shirt. The infrequent sight of them was like that of prey to a hunter. It was hell-on-leather and we used to run them down or kill our horses in the trying. It would have been a pretty sight indeed to hunt for hours and days, and then draw up at the first barricade of thorn and cactus —we would get hot after one, and believe me, we would get him, one way or another. We went after them in the thickets as fast as our horses could travel, never knowing when we would be swept out of the saddle by mesquite, never caring whether we killed ourselves, the horse or the ladinos.

"Those were hardy horses that we rode. Spanish ponies, tough as we were. From hoof to shoulder they had no hair from crashing through the brush. They had as much fun as we did. They were like human beings a-hunting in the hot breathless shadows. Their hearts would go thump, thump, against your boot as you waited. They would rear and plunge when they heard the animal breaking through in their direction. Then, stumbling and hopping and wading and crashing through cactus and catclaw and mesquite, they ran through solid walls of brush, they took the bit in their teeth after the ladino. They would have liked to catch it and shake it in their teeth like terriers. We used to let them find their own way and hold on and wait for the first bit of daylight in all that shadow. It would not be the deepest brush in the world in those foothills if you could swing a lariat. We rode hard on the tail of a ladino and we were lucky if we could flick out underhand and snare a hind leg. We had to be skillful and quick and sit back for dear life when the beast hit the end of the lariat. Sometimes he broke it as you would a string. When it held there was enough bawling and crashing about to spoil the most hard-headed siesta, and there was a clearing in that spot when the ladino got through with it. We had to snare the brute around one way or another, flip the slack and catch the other hind leg or tangle him, somehow. There weren't any rules. We had to yank him down and be out of the saddle and have him tied before he got his breath. We had some close calls, working the gravel hills. We used to wipe the sweat from our eyes, listen for the distant halloing and be off after another like men hunting stag.

"You would have snarled at us, señor, coming into camp brush-torn, our horses bathed in foam and blood, limping on two and sometimes three legs, windbroke, foundered, because you are a gringo, even if you are a good gringo, and the sentiment of your people is badly balanced. You would have snarled at our cruelty, our triumphant weariness, our heedlessness, our callous cheer, but we were just doing our job, the kind of job that gringos wouldn't do. It was dirty work, heartbreaking work, and we were nonchalant about it as old Esteban making biscuits at the chuck wagon. Besides, those horses were well the very next morning—they got over their soreness and stiffness quicker than we did.

"Can't you see Felipe in that brush and brutality, the wind and the darkness? He didn't look the part, but it was meat for him. His horse breathing hard after a ladino that frothed at the mouth and ran with stringy muscles, the huge horns shaking. His hat in his eyes, his jacket tattered, cursing his saints, with Lili scrambling after him like an urchin left behind. Can't you see Felipe—earnest and foolhardy and funnier than ever—on the crowbait horse, with that idiot Lili dangling behind him? This fallen impatient petty grandee, and we laugh to remember him, but he was killed in October of that year, in the deep *monte* of the foothills of the Little Mountains.

"The work was almost done by October. We were on the last quick sweep through the hills and out to the plains that slope to the coast, out of the hell of brush and stillness to the cool white villages and the women at home—anxious for the women like mariners from the sea—crackling through the brush like ladinos ourselves, shouting over miles in a day, in haste to be done, the devil himself stampeding our gathered herds in the night. With black night and thunder and lightning at times, but we would catch them up again at a gallop and be on as before, whooping through the foothills and thinking of the good times and tequila in the cantinas and our women at the windows.

"It was not the last thing in the world you could expect. It was not out of the ordinary, even. The pear was stamped down and there was blood on the shrubs. In an opening was Felipe's off-breed of a horse, dumb terror in its eyes,

being jerked about by a red bull that was roped to the saddlehorn. He was jerked to his knees whenever he faced the bull, and he was pulled over backwards on the saddle when they ran in opposite directions—but the strong horsehair girths held. The bull would gore him and run as if it were scared out of its wits. The bull was that quick, he could stomp the horse down and in one clear swoop be at the end of the rope and yank the horse up again. Any other time the rope would have snapped like a line.

"The bull was bellowing like one in the arena, but he wasn't mad—he was nimble and terrified, and this anchor of a horse defeated him. But what *scared* him was the body of Felipe between them, sprawling in the air like a last bad effigy of himself. Just out of the saddle, a spur caught in the fork as he had been dragged from the seat, a twist of rope around his neck as he'd fumbled in his slack, his head almost severed from the body—hanging, victim of a monstrous tug-of-war—was all that was left of Felipe. The man we laughed at, still in character, but we did not laugh—for the rope was tied to the horn, *the San Juan's way*, twisted so hard from the strain it had cut to the wood, leaving the smell of tattered leather above the gore.

"Lili was there, too—all arms and legs and lariat, beating his dumpy mare around and about, crying like a baby. We didn't rope the bull down, we rode our horses right into the bull and over him, we knocked him down with a broken shoulder, and then we were off our horses kicking him in the snout senselessly."

4

"THE DAY WE BURIED Felipe," Ernesto continued after a while, "—a wooden cross, a padre from the village, and a hole on the dry prairie—was one of the times we got into town. We never went to Pena unless we were sick or driving cattle. But this was a holiday, though the padrone gave it grudgingly enough, muttering we were not entitled to loaf on every beggar's funeral—*only on his, when he died*—so, after Chico in drink had fallen into the new-made grave and had been drawn out by a horse and lariat, we laid on with the spades and finished before Don Juan changed his mind. There was no waste of ceremony about getting away. In half an hour there was nothing around the grave but Lili hanging back like a stray dog.

"The town was a mushroom wood-built depot of the railway, a few stores, two ramshackle saloons with verandas, an acre or two of shipping pens, one of your gringo towns, not ours. The tawdry boardinghouse was hangout for a shyster, and a *juez* who was always drunk, the preacher and his woman, the respectable citizenry, including a doctor who charged two months' wage to treat the likes of us, a mule buyer, and one fat merchant with the appalling dignity of a Jew. If *we* had to sleep in town, *we* went to the pens and there, wrapped against the brisk breeze in our saddle blankets and slickers, looking out into dark brush and up at hushed stars, we hardly knew we were not in cowcamp, thank God! Even in those days, the gringos hated us.

"When we were in town it was to drink and eat. When our thirst was quenched, we would rustle an old woman to cook young goats and chickens, and we'd buy cases of canned peaches. Then we sat by to glut and laugh, washing it down with raw mescal *del gallo*. We would feast and drink for hours, and the last red bean or tortilla cleared off we would rear back and sigh and hold our lean bellies, who had never had enough to eat in our lives, well drunk, well fed.

"The San Juan was on a spree, understand. We walked down the streets with a certain air, seeming to say—look up, citizens, and welcome us! We spent our money like water in the rotten town. We had worked six months for ninety dollars, and we left the place without a penny in our pockets. Easy come, easy go—it was that way with us, señor.

"There was no disorder, we drank with no disorder in mind, though the gringos were pushing us to one side at the bar with something like contempt, talking in loud tones how the old Don had got his *greasers* so spoiled on the San Juan that now they dared to drink along besides *white* men—a bunch of swine, who had never roped a ladino in their lives or ridden a wild horse, or killed an *armed* Mexican for that matter. They were not señores like our Don Juan, although they owned land and they ran cattle. They lived in that shambles of a town called Pena, they liked it. But this was gringo country, and not Randado, or Zapata, or Roma or San Juan or any city as great as Rio Grande, and we were restrained as befitted strangers, drinking our whiskey quietly and with gusto and seeming not to notice the unfriendliness.

"The gringa ladies walked wickedly about among the men, and when a man has been in the *monte* for many months, how fresh, like the turf in *lagunas*—how sweet, like huisache blossoms—how fragrant and unutterably desirable they can be. We were like mariners in port, señor. What eyes she had! What a leg on that one! *Ah, qué chichis!* We felt we could use several women apiece, our limbs felt double looking at them, but after the first, not being in practice, we were through, *fregados*. We drank, and our minds were inflamed by so much beauty in these women. But they ignored us for the most part, moving about among the white men on their fine, proud legs, kissing and hugging the grocer, the deputy, the clerks from the market place without shame or discrimination or passion. It made your blood boil. If *this* was being civilized, it was too tame. Turning their backs and flipping up their skirts behind if a real man even touched them! The bitches, and we paid! There was a great contempt in our hearts for these bitches and bastards, for the men of these women in particular, who could not ride a bronc or tail a bull or stop a stampede, but we said no word—we drank quietly and were restrained. We didn't want any trouble with these *jotas*.

"Then Angelina came to dance—dragging her skirt from the drunkards reaching after her, picking her rather timid way to the center of the floor, and the guitars strummed livelily, a dead hush fell on the people. She was a great beauty in her time, the loveliest thing our bloodshot eyes had seen in many moons. She made the gringa women and the other sluts in that saloon look like faded roses in a prayer book. There was music in her eyes, there was magic to her lips, her bosom was a nest for the cross of gold. There was strength in her legs and shoulders to bear the love of any man. She was not a skinny wench, a painted slut, she didn't have any business there. We drank, and our eyes were bright from looking, but we were shy as boys before her dark beauty. We had been hungry for such as she, we were famished, we were afraid we would frighten her, that she would escape us.

"The musicians sang '*La Chaparita*,' the anthem of vaqueros, a song as old as the lariat and the big-horned saddle, as old as the haciendas of Sonora, and they were singing it at the top of their high voices, they were singing it for Angelina, the sweetheart of the earth. There was panic in her eyes in this gringo place, but there was laughter on her lips, and she moved like a steed that is in running form for the quarter mile. Her eyes were like a bird's, her smile was like rippling water in a pool. She was cruel, as the sun, the desert, the good cruelty that men ravish, the young cruelty. She was a woman, señor. And *gringos* listened and applauded and shouted and carried on as if this woman and the whole saloon belonged to *them—*

> "*Chaparita, si supieras*
> *cuanto te amo yo,*
> *ay, an-da-le!*
>
> "*Correspóndele a mi amor.*
> *Ay, andale! Correspóndele*
> *a mi amor.*

"They chanted it with their hog-calling voices, they improvised, they brought out rich verses as numerous as those of the '*Cucaracha*,' these *gringos;* as if the mirth, the deeds, the saga, the death and the gaiety of this song was a part of themselves and a heritage. These *gringos*"—and Ernesto spat eloquently on the dirt floor of dame Margarita's cantina—"they had no right to be moved by it," he said, "to enjoy it, to hear it. It made us mad, for it was *our* song, understand. They made sinful noises and gestures, and ogled Angelina like *padrotes,* like the pigs they were.

"But she danced the '*Chaparita*' and this was not for the pitching of quarters and the coarse pastime of gringos like the dancing of gypsies is; this was part of our people, it was passionate and beautiful and a thing that belonged to *us.* She sang for *us,* in a murmur, or she shouted from her healthy breasts, her heels and her castanets clicking together in time, her red shawl and the black dress clinging to her body like flame. She sang the '*Chaparita,*' the glorious '*Chaparita,*' señor—it was played in the capital, or an Indian village. Our fathers and their fathers had sung it to quiet the cattle at night, our mothers murmured it when we were babes. Bandits sang it, *gente* sang it, *peones* sang it. It was everything—always, lilting, insouciant, fiery, oh raw! Like the plains of Coahuila, the wolf-fanged little mountains of Randado. You could sing it till the mountains echoed, you could whisper it to a love.

"We applauded, we let out spontaneous *gritos* that raised the hair on the head. We crushed the glasses in our hands, and we hated the gringos singing:

> "*Porqué quieres amores*
> *que tengan dueños?*
>
> *Porqué quieres amores*
> *tan lejos . . .*
> *Chaparita!*

"Ah, señor," Ernesto said, and his old eyes were glad, "we were nothing but a lot of *greasers*, we were *peones*, we were dirt, señor, but we looked and we marveled at Angelina and then we knew, that even dogs have daylight. Her sweet body was a leaping flame dominated by the fury of her smile, and she was our own. Angelina! What a lovely piece! She was strong as the north winds, and yet like the winds from the south. You could not stop her, one so fanatical; you could not touch her, she was a dream. Her magnificent body was that of a woman, a tigress, what can I say—an angel, Angelina! She was fierce, with the dim suffering eyes; she was glad, with the cruel mouth. She was violent, she was lovely—a vaquero's woman, a woman born in the white villages, the answer to us, the slake to our thirst.

"We beat the time with our boots, our spurs jingling, and we kicked the silver the gringos threw at her feet back under the tables angrily. It made us angry to see such a woman in such a place, but we desired her, nonetheless. The guitars strummed louder and louder, and our greedy eyes were wide. Her dress was torn, her hair all down, and she kicked up her legs like a *yegua*. *Ay, ay!* We fell to quarreling, and we spilled the whiskey at the bar. Understand, señor, it was quarreling among ourselves. But this deputy told us to get out, he called us hard names. And then, we forgot our quarrel and Angelina and the music and the whiskey. The *coraje* came flushing up in our faces so that we could fairly taste it. Some one slashed the deputy across the mouth with a quirt for his insolence, and everyone in the room sprang at bay. The gringos scuttered together like *animales*. Lázaro gave a fetch-call as we stepped down from the rail, and the others from San Juan in the town came galloping as fast as their ponies would go. They rode their horses right into the saloon.

"The gringo with the red welt rising in his face did not move. Pablo stalked in front of the rest, roaring. He foamed at the mouth, his beard fairly bristled, and to hear him one would have thought him terrible. But we laughed, because they were frightened, like city men.

"Angelina stood on the bar, with tangled hair, her eyes snapping, screaming like a drunk woman. We were spoiling for a fight, we outdid each other insulting them. Tomás wanted to duel any three at thirty paces with rifles. El Gordo broke the kerchief at his neck and fawned on a large red-faced man; but gringos don't like cold steel. When the man saw the blade in El Gordo's hand, the bandana in his teeth, and the glint in his wheedling eyes, he turned sick and white. And El Gordo almost caressing the man with affection . . . *ay, gringos*. We harried them with the foulest names in the Spanish tongue, we pleaded and spat in their faces, but all for *nothing, para nada!* I tell you they were city men.

"We let them go with a hoot of derision, and the music struck up and someone grabbed Angelina and they played the '*Chaparita.*' On with the lilting, good '*Chaparita,*' on with the '*Chaparita*' as if nothing had happened. The shouting was heard all over the town and the gringos pulled in their shutters and barred the doors. We slugged the bartender, naturally, and emptied his whiskey-keg, chasing it down with hot beer.

"There would be hell to pay tomorrow—what with fancy sheriffs and perhaps the blustering vigilantes and complaints to high heaven and bills for wreckage, and old Don Juan would be black and blue as a *grullo* horse, he would be that mad, but he was a good padrone, and he'd fix everything—and tomorrow was tomorrow and this was today and the world was our own. On with the '*Chaparita*' —bring out the ladies, turn up the lights; play the '*Chaparita,*' over and over again. We drank and we sang and we shouted until the dim of dawn. And then we were on our horses and out in the open country and we were back and put in a day's work over many a chuckle and memory."

5

There might be something wrong with me, but I could never help loving the Mexicans. All of them, good and bad, because they were human to a vivid degree. My principal regret about the years I wasted in the southwest is that with the padrone complex and carrying the White Man's Burden, I had very little chance to be human with them. I could only look at them wistfully and come away sadly, wishing at times that I could be a Mexican. I have always wanted to write about the Mexicans, improve the relations between our races, but anybody who tried to do that in the southwest fifteen years ago was despised by his own people *and* the Mexicans.

I really liked what I saw of them so well that if I had to be poor, dirt poor—and it were possible, if I were allowed —I think I would rather live among the Mexicans than the gringos. The Mexicans have a way of being poor with dignity. And what blessed contrary vassals they were, I practically worked for *them!* They served me well on the Jesús María, I can remember them only with regard, but they were characters. They treated me with consideration, and they were honest as the day is long, I believe they actually liked me, but I could not help but feel that they had adopted me. It was nice, though, to be liked by them.

When I gave up ranching finally, they would not let me leave like an ordinary person, they even put on a sort of *aloha*. It was so ridiculous and sincere, I was almost touched by their blackmail into staying. They didn't want me to go. The women and children had come with absurd little presents, holding their rosaries and supplicating that I stay—Oh quaint pastoral conceit!—and in its fashion that was a testimonial. And the vaqueros, those fine horsemen and good companions, and by your leave always, men to spill the blood of your enemies—*allow me, excuse me, padrone,* they used to say for the privilege—these had followed me down the road at a gallop, singing, shouting *Adiós, ay, Juanito! Adiós, compañero* . . . like characters in a horse-opera, and some of them had cried.

It was all very charming, I felt I was seeing uncommonly fine acting for amateur theatricals, but I couldn't get away from feeling it was unreal—I even had a sneaking idea that I was leaving all these good people stranded in my own make-believe. As long as I had been their padrone, they could be as extravagant and human as they wished, but when I left they had to start acting like *pelados* again, taking crap off of *white* men. So perhaps the Mexicans did hate to see me leave, and it was a dirty trick to imagine them and then leave them high and dry in their parts, even if for a while they'd had a blessed holiday from their peonage. They might even have appreciated me, for they always treated me like the young padrone. They made the role easy to play, these frustrated Thespians, and perhaps it was the only one I ever acted convincingly, but what props I had, what a stage, what prompters, and what a cast! I was absurd as the Mexicans, for there was a time when I actually believed, in this topsy-turvy world, the Jesús María and the southwest was the only place I really belonged.

I was only the figurehead, understand, the Mexicans would never allow me to be anything but their padrone. And that can be a lonely mixed blessing, for though they keep a straight face and a humble mien around the padrone they really think that gringos are great fools, and at heart the Mexicans are communists. When they have the *coraje,* they are even anarchists. They liked me, but I could feel their innate disrespectful drollery, their slapstick ribaldry unuttered, the contempt in their spirit, their gorgeous dignity—and I felt somehow that I existed by their leave, mind you. I felt I might even awake some morning and find myself demoted, a full-blown revolution on the Jesús María. I have felt their unspoken reservations following when my back was turned, and so pertinently that I have wished I was a buck private. I never had anything but consideration from them, they were nicer to me than to any gringo in the country, but I have felt like their own hidalgos feel at times, that I was an unpopular headmaster in a boy's school.

There is something of Puck in the Mexican. He will give you the shirt off his back, and is always ready to take yours, which is a much better one. He can haunt the gringo, hex him, and he knows it—it is something we will not admit for shame or pride. He can turn you inside out, make you feel like a fool or a prince, he can hate you silently and have you wondering about Doomsday, and he has a way of looking at Money that makes the Capitalists shudder. He won't stay bought, he will do anything as a favor, but for Money he renders himself like a handful of dust.

You've never got him over a barrel, he can live on prickly pear and rabbit, there has always been a Depression for him. It's all right if he adopts you, but then you haven't any private life; as his friend or patron, there is no fiercer light beats down on any throne, you are his mother and his father and his brother and his wet nurse and his legend to make and gossip about to his heart's content—*and you had better be good*—and a politician and diplomat as well, a bondsman to keep him out of jail, and he even goes around saying his padrone can lick your padrone, until you wish sometimes you could lay down the White Man's Burden with a sigh.

You wish you could be a Mexican yourself. Like José, for instance, that *pendejo,* he lives the full life. He was the most amiable gold-brick I ever knew. He later adjusted himself to American ways when he left the ranch to work in the oilfields, and now he lives in a half-timber, half-*caliche* house in Randado with real wooden floors, and he is a Capitalist. He works for a large oil company, and he is what the gringos call spoiled. He makes too much money for a *greaser,* and his family have a Singer Sewing Machine and a radio, and José has a vast amount of poor relations that sprawl around his little house like fixtures, and address him respectfully as Don José and complain of the food. They even threaten to leave him unless he has *cabrito* more often. The very number of

José's poor relations attest to his prosperity, for with the Mexicans wealth is something that is shameful unless it is shared. And why should the relatives work, when José is fool enough to be a Capitalist? They were his friends when he was poor, and now they are his friends and relations. José accepts them with good grace, because with his sewing machine and radio and poor relations he is a Success—and of course, he has seven or eight children, so many that his wife has to count them in and out of their second-hand automobile when they drive to Pena.

Yet, at times José is not content, he doesn't like being the padrone around his little establishment. He realizes that he makes good money, but he does not have the leisure or the irresponsibility that his friends and relations enjoy, and he gets tired of them putting the hex on him. When his patience wears thin he gets the *coraje* like any other man, and he almost loses his job because the oil company finds that José is not a good handyman when he has the *coraje*. It is then that he wishes he had a padrone to put up with his temperament, or better still, that he did not have a job. He will have the door-handles working left-handed, he will putty inside the windows, and the faucets will drip. Not deliberately, understand, but because he has the *coraje*, the terrible ennui.

A house or yard or the garage or machine shop where José has cleaned with the ennui looks as if the Little People had been around in a playful mood. And in these quirks, when José is not philosophical and is lamenting perhaps the burden of his in-laws and the installments he has to pay on the radio and the automobile like any gringo, or he has had to bail a nephew out of jail like any padrone, an incident that regularly adds to José's prestige and is excitement while it lasts but nonetheless aggravating and costs money—when José is indulging himself and his whimsical humors and regretting the day he left the Jesús María to become a Capitalist, he has been known to get drunk and beat his wife and call his employer a *chinga-madre* and to complain in the cantinas, that it was a hard trade, the Capitalist's trade.

If there is one characteristic predominate in José it is that of humanity, for, like all honest men, he hates to work. In fact, he loathes work, he would rather be sitting around the cantinas, doing nothing. He used to practice a little desultory plumbing in his spare time, and although José was the most undependable Mexican in the country, all the ranchers had to depend on him for their plumbing. They couldn't hire anybody else, or he would get mad and not come when they really needed him—not that he ever came promptly, anyway. He always arrived two or three days late, rather grandly with an assistant, who called him *maestro,* and what he did to your toilet or sink was done with much ceremony, because José dearly loved the paraphernalia of his trade.

You had to keep after José, and because he was droll, it was almost impossible to find him when you needed him. His principal vice was procrastination, but his promises in themselves were a form of politeness. He didn't want to hurt your feelings, or it was the plain *pendejo* in José, the poetic justice in the Mexican that seeks to avenge itself on supposedly insupportable social systems in trifling ways, or maybe it was just his manner of showing you he was not your man any more than you were his, but José would promise to come when your toilet overflowed like a tide or a broken pipe flooded the kitchen floor, and promptly and in almost a princely manner, forget all about it. Or he would be grievously late, for to him punctuality was the courtesy of kings only. When in great wrath you finally ran into him, and meanwhile had learned to be a fair amateur plumber yourself, he pointed this out to you politely, and was usually so charming and had such an air of injury that you had bothered him over such a little matter, that you ended by buying him a beer. You couldn't help but like José.

And you take Chávez and Luro, those clowns. People say that Mexicans don't have a sense of humor, but this Luro is a comedian unconsciously. He had the biggest shotgun wedding in Jim Hogg and Zapata counties, and where the rape had taken place a deputy said it looked like a couple of bulls had been fighting. She was a fine upstanding woman, and Luro made her a good husband, after his fashion. He finally lost her through an attack of the colic, he could never understand why. She was just spirited away in the night. She was a fine buxom woman in the prime of life—fat, like he liked 'em.

The night she died she and Luro had their regular supper of enchiladas dripping with cheese and covered with chopped raw onions—she could surely cook enchiladas, Luro said, you could taste them for several days afterwards—an omelette with *chiltipiquin,* which is an intolerable wild pepper, one of which can make a tureen of soup unpalatable, and pinto beans with steak, toasted tortillas cooked in hogfat, goat cheese on the side, coffee extract without sugar or cream because Luro likes his coffee rank, and his wife said sugar was fattening—and nothing else. Then they went to a cinema in Zapata, and Elena had a couple of bags of popcorn, a sack of peanuts, two chocolate bars, nothing out of the ordinary, understand, washed down with two bottles of cream soda. When they got home, she had a snack of avocado with mayonnaise, and since she had a touch of indigestion, she had a spoonful of cayenne pepper which is good for the colic, and after that she felt so well, she heated up some chili con carne left over from lunch and they ate this together and went to bed and slept hard, both of them.

That is, until about two o'clock, when his wife woke up hollering bloody murder and Jesus and Mary and Madre de Dios, and for a doctor like a woman possessed, and died before the doctor even got there. Luro could never understand why, but he wasn't heartbroken. She was just spirited away, he said.

6

CHÁVEZ AND LURO have come up in the world since they worked for the Jesús María. They are now by way of being cattle buyers and horse dealers *sans peur et sans reproche*. You are safe betting like they do on a horse, because they don't bet on anything but cinches. Luro is a guy six feet three and weighs almost three hundred pounds, none of it fat; he used to be able to hold a bronc by one ear and saddle it with the other hand. He can split a table with his fist, and open beer bottles with his teeth, and when he speaks in a whisper the rafters shake in the dim cantinas, and I remember him coming into camp *crudo* many a time and waking everybody in the dead of night exclaiming in a stage whisper that was loud enough to stampede the cattle how damned good the cool water in the *jolla* was. . . . *Ah, qué bueno, qué bueno,* he used to say over and over as if he were drinking beer.

Luro had a child-like faith in Chávez, who is the brains of their eternal partnerships, but he is always buying and trading, forever trying to get—well, to get even with Chávez. Luro and Chávez live rather grandly now in Zapata, where everything is theirs for the asking. They have their finger in politics because the Mexicans vote solidly as Chávez advises and the brawny Luro threatens, they are great cardplayers, and since they must bear the mark of successful men, they own cantinas.

Chávez and Luro walk the streets of Zapata every Sunday afternoon, when the Mexicans come to town, and they are padrones in little, casting an official eye over the new fillies, these middle-aged blades, guessing the weight and height of these country girls with great dignity. I used to watch with amusement as these two gallants went swaggering by of a Sunday afternoon in Zapata. I would be drinking coffee in the little restaurant that Chávez owns on the main square, and while his wife filled my cup with the rank coffee she would complain, *Ah, qué viejos!* She looked at them rather helplessly, with a secret admiration, because all Mexican women are proud of trifling husbands.

The Mexicans are a warm friendly lovable people, or rather, they used to be. I remember even our Negro cook, Ben, became a human being around the Mexicans, although at heart he was an arrogant Negro and he goaded them unmercifully. Ben was a two-hundred pound uppity Negro from Austin who used to work for our family there, and he wouldn't let anybody in the southwest forget it. He treated most of the whites in the county cavalierly, he was one to keep them in their proper places, and where they would have lynched any other smart Negro, they merely pretended Ben was rude to everybody else but not to the likes of them, although they had a hard time pretending.

Ben got the upper hand on you, and he put a foot in your soul. He was the essence of black majesty. He used to talk my arm off, because he and I were the only ones on the Jesús María who spoke English, and I have listened to him while he rubbed his back against the doorjamb while he told me a few things about women. That you could always tell a woman's age by the wrinkles in her neck, that every woman has her own scent if she doesn't kill it with perfume, and the principal thing for a man to do is to marry the woman who loves him, not the woman *he* loves. He had some good takeoffs of pedestrians in New York, where Ben had been a chauffeur once, and the Mexicans used to bust a gut laughing at him. He was another character I left stranded in that make-believe, a very strange Negro, because the Mexicans adopted him, too, and he never went back to his own people.

And there was a character I remember in Zapata named Lázaro, well-named he was, a man who had been everything from a pimp to a revolutionist. Lázaro was born in Mier, and he had an unreasonable dread of the Immigration, though he had been in our country for thirty years. But then Lázaro had things on his conscience: he was known to have bootlegged in his day, and his mother was a fierce old woman who shot it out with revenue officers. Lázaro had also been a thief, when he had to be. But few of these things discredited Lázaro as a man—the only reason he was held in contempt by the Mexicans, though he was a liar and *sinvergüenza* among other things, was because of the fact that Lázaro wore the horns. The Mexicans are very sensitive about having the horns put on them, or at least, in a manner so that it shows.

And that stallion Luro had done it unfairly, while Lázaro was doing a stretch on the prison farm. The Mexicans thought he should put a knife in Luro's ribs, or at least dry-gulch him, but Lázaro acted in this matter in a strangely civilized manner, very unlike a Mexican—it might be he had not dared avenge this insult to his questionable honor because he was fresh out of prison and always rather a stranger in a strange land, this the Mexicans could understand, but what they could never understand or forgive in Lázaro was the fact that he took the woman back. *Because he loved her,* he said—and they would listen, and spit eloquently on the floor. That wasn't any reason, that was no way for a man to act. And if he married another, Lázaro argued, how could he be sure she wouldn't be unfaithful, too, the next time he was sent up the river? Girls were all *putas,* nowadays. You didn't want a virgin any more, you were lucky to marry a girl that didn't have the gonorrhea.

Ah, the Mexicans can be children, and sometimes the Mexicans can be nice children, especially when they take care of their halfwits. Every village keeps its halfwits at home, the Mexicans would never be so inhuman as to send anybody away from his *patria,* his home. They tease these halfwits, they are amused by their antics, but they are good to them. In fact, they treat them something like sacred lunatics at times, and are superstitious about them. We had a couple of these unfortunates in the village, nor would anybody think of sending them to an asylum. That would be a disgrace to the Jesús María, even though one of the idiots was not properly ours. We called that one the Mad Monk, and he had long hair and wild eyes, he used to stand in the cobbled street and wave at everybody like an official greeter. Before he came to the Jesús María he had belonged twelve years to Don Carlos, trying to pay off a twenty dollar debt, and when his peonage was canceled he had come to the Jesús María to retire.

We also called him the Mad Monk because he spent what little money he earned or begged in the village burning candles in the chapel, and the priest that came on Sundays to hold services used to lay a kindly hand on the poor fellow's head, and this so touched the Mad Monk that he wept. And in the dim afternoons, the poor fellow would look up the street towards the twilight, and say that it stretched right on, without a break, through the Little Mountains, and that he would walk, some day, up that street into the twilight that led to God.

Calistro was the other idiot, and at times he was a rude sort of minstrel. But principally he was idiotic. If he knew you well enough he would come riding furiously out of the brush on his broomstick horse, and draw up in a cloud of dust. Every village seemed to have one of these broomstick idiots, it was their favorite aberration. Calistro would ride up to you and doff his Robin Hood hat with the brim cut off, bringing his broomstick to stand like a spirited horse, and then he would be away without a word, using a rawhide lash on his own buttocks. He would disappear in the huisache groves in a frenzy of make-believe. He was a very old man, barefoot, with an unwrinkled face. He was more neglected than the Mad Monk, and not as sacred.

One day Luro found him in the brush with worms in

his hand. Luro had a hell of a time catching him, and then he had to hold Calistro while he doctored the hand with Peerless Worm Medicine and painted the wound against flyblows. The creosote solution evidently burned like coal-oil, because when Luro let him up, Calistro ran around in a panic, like a small child will run when it is hurt. And when I think of that little incident, my heart is wrung with pity, and why do I remember such things, Calistro having worms in his hand, or the Mad Monk not having any teeth and the trouble he had chewing and how he went behind the houses to eat, or the brush and the brutality and the bitter beauty and the raw humor—only the vivid things, the pathetic things, the hateful things in a land where even the peace was troubled—why do I remember these things? Perhaps there was something wrong with my perspective, even then. Or else the country was, as I have always maintained, splendid and mad.

7

T**HE WHOLE LAND'S QUEER**, everything about it, everybody in it. You take that fantastic horse cavalry down the river a ways, they were around the Mexican border for years, like something out of a period movie. They were the last American horse cavalry, stationed on the Rio Grande at one of those antiquated posts built during the Mexican War, living in our God-forsaken country something like exiles—all of them, officers and men, rather having been in the Philippines or foreign service than on the Mexican border. It was more foreign than any foreign country, and not as pleasant. It had all the drawbacks of the tropics without the *dolce far niente*.

The cavalry had nothing to do, not even patrol, they were just stuck in that antiquated fort like an American Foreign Legion. There were no buffalo-hunters or Indians, but they were on a frontier, just the same. They were characters in an old silent movie. They had been first stationed here during the war of 1917, and they were not mechanized nor the fort abandoned until 1930—it was a mean post in a hard little town with few people who spoke English. It was hot arid country desolate as the Valley of Despond, with even the Rio Grande a trickle in the summer you could wade across. A sullen forgotten unlovely spot, and I will not tell its name—but the cavalry was there, with nothing to do, and that with a vengeance.

It had been rather incredible to see this crack cavalry in our lost world, these troopers were out of place, and on manoeuvres through the brush, the ranks dashing along, or pulling down to a trot in a cloud of dust and with an archaic clanking of sabres, handling like strange music that was conducted by the baton of their colonel's hand, these men were a sight to see. It was quaint, to use an understatement, to see the lean troopers with their campaign hats tipped up, their faces burnt by inclement sun, hundreds of horsemen able to ride, playing soldier—it had been a fine sight, it made the heart rise, but it was something out of focus, it didn't make sense, it all belonged to the time of Richard Harding Davis.

They hung on incongruously in our land, they seemed like a ghost cavalry, out of time, out of mind, something the War Department had forgotten, overlooked in the orders of the day or the year. The officers of this cavalry were quite old and gray, and most of the troopers seemed to have been stationed here forever. Only an occasional young officer was sent from West Point or a recruit from Riley, men trained for cavalry replacements but almost anomalous in the twentieth century. The War Department kept the regiment in strength, although it seemed to begrudge the fact these men were mortal, and therefore died or were disabled or were retired. They were just tin soldiers stationed on the Mexican border, left over from the time of Pershing and Villa.

The War Department wanted them there like stage effects. It wasn't funny, it was pathetic. This cavalry went about their forgotten tasks with old equipment, dressed as if by theatrical costumers, they practiced the outmoded tactics of the Spanish-American War, and to give our lost world on the Mexican border credit, it is a good country for cavalry, any time. In our brush with the cactus growing higher than a man on horseback, a regiment of cavalry could stand off the Republic of Mexico—or for that matter, if Wheeler's Third Georgia Cavalry had come with my grandfather and harbored themselves in this part of the southwest, using guerrilla methods, the War between the States would still be going on in a bushwhacking way. Airplanes cannot strafe here, or infantry move except at a disadvantage, and cavalry can live off the country—it would smash anything that entered the hinterland, it could outlast an invasion, what a place to hide! And every man in the lost world, every man on horseback, is a bandit or a hidalgo.

They were the last American horse cavalry—these were the men trained in flank and frontal attack on swift horses, brave as the Polish lancers under Murat, obedient as the English at Balaklava, but in the Rio Grande country they were doing nothing but hiding in the brush. They were a fine regiment in a fine tradition, die-hards to a man, but that was their trouble, their fame was in the past, they had outlived their service and their glory. The last time they had served was with Pershing in Chihuahua. Since then, they had been inactive and for so long, they had become anonymous.

They went about their make-believe, lean and hard and in condition, waiting for some return from Elba like the Guard that dies but never surrenders. Most of them were old enough for retirement. The men in their tradition had died with the yellow-haired Custer, they had stopped the *lanceros* of Santa Anna at Resaca de la Palma as that Mexican cavalry came thundering along, and it was with pride they pointed to a record of having fought on both sides in the War between the States, some with McClellan and others with Jeb Stuart, but after participating in the battle of San Juan Hill and a desultory service in the Philippines, they had come to this dump-heap, the last of their battle flags were draped in the mess, and they were a horse cavalry forgotten, a period of the early part of the century —stuck on the Mexican border, a ghostly cavalcade you could rub your eyes at seeing and not believe, their tradition a long time dying.

What made it worse, during all the period they were stationed here, and it certainly was long enough to have become acquainted, they were received with scant respect by the sullen natives. The natives acted as if they had been invaded by this cavalry, they were all for having it withdrawn and they wrote letters to their congressmen. The Mexicans and the gringos acted during the entire time the regiment was with them as if they were being occupied, but at times the lost world is inclined to forget it is part of the United States.

There was little diversion for the troopers, nothing for them to do but get drunk and into trouble, they wasted their leisure and they died of the boredom. And drinking themselves senseless in the drab cantinas like men in torrid climates will, dreaming perhaps of going back to the United States someday, there was a great deal of discontent among the men, and even mutiny. A lot of the troopers went over the hill. Some of the non-coms deserted every time a revolution in Mexico came along, and were given high rank in the Mexican Army. In fact, there was so much desertion, with the other side of the Rio Grande looking so much greener to the troopers in their boredom, that the War Department took cognizance and acted on this fact some ten years after the first World War and began the red-taped proceedings to have the post evacuated and this last horse cavalry mechanized.

These men were glad to go, they had outlived their usefulness, but it had been a sad sight to see the final review—the colonel with tears running down his leathery cheeks, and the troopers passing with their guidons waving, and sabres flashing in the air, and not an enlisted man with an eye that was not moist, either. They were tough boys, but sentimental, and they were in love with a Lost Cause. They didn't give a damn about the post, or the years they had wasted, but they hated to see good horse cavalry mechanized. They had been cavalry for so long they had forgotten how to be anything else, and in especial, mechanics. It had been sad to watch that last review; it was something that nobody in this country will ever see again.

The troopers were all right. So were the officers of that hard-bitten post. I knew them all. They played polo— even the enlisted men had teams—and the Jesús María was, principally, a horse ranch, so we took our horses down to play the cavalry at polo, about twice a month.

We'd have played more often, but it took horses and men a couple of weeks to get the kinks out between matches. They were rough, and I suppose it was a good thing we never had matches with the enlisted men—that was murder. They fairly killed each other, and sometimes in their rage they beat each other over the head with the mallets. The cavalry vastly enjoyed polo, it was one of the things that kept the troopers from going mad on that desolate outpost, and the whole regiment would turn out for the games we played with the officers, and root and cheer, mostly for us. There were seven or eight officers who alternated on the Army team, and our ranch outfit was made of Chávez and Juan Calvo and myself and usually some vaquero we took along to play Number One, with nothing to do but ride off—which he did so effectively that in his enthusiasm he often rode his opponent into the automobiles, until it was explained to him at great length that this was not necessary and incurred a penalty.

The cavalry were rough as we were, and they had finer teamwork, but no matter how wild the Army got, my vaqueros thought it was a lark. Chávez and Juan Calvo always rode green horses—we used these matches to train our prospects—and it was amazing the bumps they were able to take, and to see Chávez and Juan pick up these green horses and bounce them right back at the officers. Sometimes they rode horses so green they were rank, they had to seesaw them around, but that did not keep Chávez and Juan from kicking out, from dashing in where angels feared to tread. I have seen them on horses that would not even stop, much less handle, and they would get on the line of ball and kick wide-open into a pocket of three men—I used to just close my eyes and shudder, and if the

Army did not get out of the way, two or three horses and players went down in a scramble. As for myself, in these little games between the United States Cavalry and the Jesús María, I had more falls in one day than I would have playing tournament polo in a month. It was like a damned rodeo, or hockey on horseback. The Army sure hated to lose, but they were good guys. They were a little cracked, but good guys.

Especially Jerry Calahan from Baltimore, and Peter McBride from New York, two young officers out of West Point, men my own age—they hadn't been at the station a year when I knew them, and they thought it was fine. They hadn't been there long enough to get used to the boredom or calloused to the country, because the first year is always the hardest. They got in trouble before the year was out. It is incredible, but do you know that these young men, friends of mine, actually had a duel, the first occurrence of the kind in the American Army since the Civil War? It was strange, and a scandalous thing to hush up, and over a woman in the town.

They were two young men who came of fourth-generation Army, very correct families. Jerry and Pete had never expected to be dumped in a hole like this antiquated post on the Mexican border, and they were certainly not prepared for the society of native women nor was there anything in Regulations about Conchita. She was a little vivid for them to start with—they had been raised to believe that women were to be honored and had in them something of Pollyanna, and that officers were gentlemen. They thought the señoritas were fine and wholesome, and they would have been shocked to learn otherwise. Jerry and Pete thought it was fine to be stationed in that quaint border town, it was like something out of a book, and the girls were lovely, bright-eyed and smiling, or that is what they wrote home—fetching in high heels with beautiful legs, shameless flirts, but they were too much the gentlemen to mention that part—and there was no harm in the señoritas, they were always singing, like canaries. And the ones that weren't whores, were practicing to be.

Conchita danced in a cantina and was just part of the masquerade to them, she had a heart of gold, and came really from a fine old Spanish family. They started making excuses for her right away, they were ingenuous, they might even have had ideas of marrying the girl! They were, at any rate, rivals for the affections of that young whore. She was daring and provocative, for like the rest of the tawny, black-haired, black-eyed señoritas she was adept at pleasing men, and she wore a gold cross between her breasts that were like flags at half-mast. There is nothing like that cross of gold to set off the breasts.

Conchita was a girl for Jerry and Pete to write home about; they were attracted by her beauty in that background, and she wore a red rose behind her ear. You didn't have to be bored, or to have lost your principles to look twice at Conchita. Everything is relative, and she looked good in that little border town. She was rather delicious in that drab land, she could chatter and laugh and make a man feel like the cock of this world. She had a mature figure, but the child-like face, that blend of innocence and allure that gives a man the delusion he holds most fondly, that he is continually seducing Innocence. She was thoughtless and cruel and wicked as a child.

It was all right that the two innocents fell for her, but what remains to be told is something out of a bad horse-opera. Conchita was nothing the gringos would not have taken by force, but these two fine West Pointers, hot-house products, utterly guileless, fine lads, honor-bright and brave in a useless cavalry, they wanted to marry the girl! It was too bad the colonel hadn't known about it in time, he would have sent Conchita packing.

Perhaps in a way this country was Adventure to Jerry and Pete—it had the background for Romance. The crooked streets of this Mexican-American town were cobbled, and the houses built at crazy angles, stacked and leaning and haphazard like dwellings in the Land of Oz, and in these very United States the windows bellied out in the street and behind iron bars, like Christian slaves, were the dark-eyed black-haired señoritas, roses in their hair, and beaux looking up at them and strumming on guitars. Jerry and Pete were surprised and delighted by the novelty of the town, the activity in the streets during the day and the night—even assassins seemed to lurk in the alleys after dark—and the only time that the place was dead, with all the natives and animals asleep, when it looked like something enchanted out of 'La Belle au Bois Dormant,' was during the sacred siesta. But at four o'clock the citizens always awoke, they struggled alive as from the effects of drugs, and there was renewed activity in the plaza, the shouting and gregarious Mexicans carrying on their business with holiday spirit.

It was good as something out of a play. Oh the large happy leisure of these charming people! The vaqueros covered with dust clattered down the cobbled street, though their horses were unshod and stepped daintily— and these careless souls with the jingling spurs and the long tapaderos and the rawhide chaps, how they made cracks good-naturedly at everybody they saw, heaping abuse on the poor head of the ancient who delivered water in a barrel-wagon drawn by a burro, casting their lariats at all stray dogs, greeting the unseemly and the dignified and even the soldiers with ribald and barbaric extravagance, and offering their services to every female, young and old and ugly and beautiful, who looked out a window or door. Jerry and Pete almost envied these carefree people, they liked the Mexicans, they would have been friendly with the folk in the lost world, but the people in that particular town would not have it, they acted like the Army had invaded them.

The Mexicans were always silent for an unmistakable instant when the two young officers entered a cantina, and the gringos scowled at them. The gringos mope in these cantinas along the border, they look like they've got dyspepsia, or as if, *válgame Dios!* the Mexicans say, they have something on their consciences. They are like exiles and glum, always complaining of the Mexicans, and that this is part of the United States, and they have to speak Spanish like they were in Mexico. It was a long time before Jerry and Pete realized how unfriendly the gringos were, and if they tried to be friendly with the Mexicans, the Mexicans would shut up politely, or act as if they had been waiting a long time for this, and now they were not bored by anything.

The first visits my friends made in the town must have been literal sightseeing tours, though—it had been a lark, just like Mexico, Jerry Calahan had written to his mother. There was a quaint square. It was deserted, and more like a city dump than an easygoing Mexican plaza, as I remember it, cluttered with junk, neglected and weed-

grown. It overlooked the Rio Grande from the ungracious bluffs. And in the very center of this tiny square had been a carousel—in sad disrepair, the harness all cracked and the canopy frayed to let in the sunlight and the rain, and yes, at night the very moonlight was strange and entattered about this forsaken carousel—there were only six horses, and about this tiny carousel there had been a curious legend, I remember.

It was said that one night a dozen years before, when this little carousel had been bright and painted and turned to a lively tune, a drunken vaquero from the unknown ends of this weird land had climbed on the blue horse—it is still a blue horse, they say, but faded like old denim— and had roared around in glee, roweling with the huge Mexican spurs, taking slugs from his bottle of mescal and waving the bottle in the air, spoiling all the children's fun and bringing the *policía* down the street, until even in his drunken condition he realized he was out of order. He realized this, or at last he tired of the silly diversion, but when he stepped down from that same wooden horse, he had not gone three steps in the plaza, until he disappeared. All the people in the square saw it, and the *policía*.

He just blinked out, and he never was heard of, he was not seen again. And the Mexicans being the charming and superstitious people they are, had deserted that little square, and its tiny carousel had been abandoned like an accursed thing. Old crones said that anyone who rode the blue horse, who stepped down from that ramshackle merry-go-round in the deserted square, would not get to the street corner before he was gone, just like that, and nobody would hear of him again. Even the Old Men hurried by the place at night. And it was curious, too, that none of the troopers, being mostly Irish and believing in the Little People and all sorts of things—but who were brave as lions when they were drunk and would ask the colonel to have a drink with them—that none of these troopers, drunk or sober, ever gave that blue horse a ride. It just pranced there gallantly in the deserted square as did the other five horses, and the tiny carousel made no sound.

I wish I could make Jerry and Pete disappear like the vaquero who rode the blue horse. Conchita was a bitch, and she played them against one another in fiendish and innocent and childish delight, she it was who gave them the kiss of death. It is an old love story, and it has been told before, so the details aren't necessary. And one never gets the straight of these affairs, and certainly the girl was too frightened at the inquest to talk—though at the investigation the Army prosecutor had all but quartered and drawn her, she would not talk. It was a sad affair for all concerned, and a disgrace to this useless cavalry, for it ended with finding Jerry and Pete on a lonely road, dead in their own blood with pistols in their hands.

Don't ask me why they did it, don't ask me what makes the gringo go haywire on the Mexican border, all I can say is that something seems to get in the gringo's blood down here, strange and gorgeous and exotic like marihuana and men do inexplicable things. It was the first duel in the Army since the Civil War! And over such a creature as Conchita—they wanted to marry the girl—whom any lout of a gringo would take like a whore, but then, she probably never understood the restrained young officers who were in love with her so honorably, the Mexican girl in the cantinas not being made in that fashion. The gringos say that all you've got to do is throw them down, and the more they holler, the better they like it.

8

And who could have been stranger than my great-uncle Beverly? He didn't stay in this country, he just passed through, but he was a character. My great-uncle Beverly was an adventurer, a famous duelist, one of the last soldiers-of-fortune in the Trelawney fashion, and never any more ridiculous than a duelist can be. His superiors in the Confederate Army bent backwards not to offend his exotic and dangerous sense of Honor, they thought he was crazy, and maybe he was. My grandfather was a better man, he was wounded six times humbly fighting for the Lost Cause, he fought on foot, he was a more worthy and kindlier person than my great-uncle, he had more character, but since only the poets and soldiers live vividly, I will tell you of my great-uncle Beverly.

He led a brigade of cavalry for Johnston, as that unsung and capable commander fell back stunned and outnumbered on Atlanta. Great-uncle's cavalry had swept back the pincers of Sherman's army time and again to let the bedraggled Confederates withdraw to fight another day. It was one of the greatest retreats in history. It was one of those blessed campaigns where—there was more glory in defeat than in victory. It had been just the thing for great-uncle Beverly, he led his cavalry blithely, with consummate dash—there had been no odds too great for his troopers to attack, and it was known that Sherman was indignant that an English partisan was turning the flanks of an American army, whipping the sluggish infantry cavalierly on the backsides with sabres, and Sherman possibly would have hung my great-uncle Beverly if he had captured him. Perhaps that is one reason my great-uncle never surrendered at all.

There was no nonsense about great-uncle Beverly's dueling. My grandfather used to say it started at Sandhurst with a cadet slapping my great-uncle's face, and that had made a killer of him. He could never get over the indignity of it, for great-uncle Beverly had a right royal complex. He shot the cadet through the mouth, in the Bois at Paris. Then, his British military career nipped in the bud, he had come to Georgia to be a planter with grandfather. He was a very elegant and quarrelsome young man, but so were the Southern Gentlemen.

His first duel in Atlanta was with a captain of militia named Sawtelle. A crack rifleman, and blustery, but it was great-uncle who put a rifle bullet between the captain's eyes. My great-uncle would fight any kind of duel except the ones that involved personal contact. After his duel with the captain, according to the peculiar hot-blooded punctilio of Georgia, he had been challenged by Sawtelle's brother and him too my great-uncle killed, and then a

brother-in-law had died in the same fashion for Honor's Sake, bringing the list of widows to three, and five years later—while the scion of that undistinguished family was coming of age, and great-uncle here and there had brought his score to twelve and was fast running out of competition —my great-uncle Beverly had to kill the last of the Sawtelle family, it was said, reluctantly. Of course, grandfather said that was all twaddle about the fine sentiment. For great-uncle Beverly had been one of the south's last cavaliers, the Beau Ideal of a ridiculous southern chivalry, he went everywhere in his wizard's cloak of Death, and if he did not enjoy it, then I can only think of that lonely cavalier with a queer catch in my throat; and, blood of my blood, I am sorry for that poor gentleman. Grandfather always said it was a great pity, and a great inconvenience, to be a Southern Gentleman.

When the Civil War was over, but had not been settled except at Appomattox, neither great-uncle nor my grandfather surrendered—they went to Texas, where they fought with the last Confederate forces under Kirby Smith, and when that general gave up, great-uncle went to Mexico. My grandfather went along as far as the border, but he liked this country between the Nueces and the Rio Grande, it looked enough like Mexico for him, so he settled near Randado, buying his land of the Viscayas with ill-gotten but thumping Yankee dollars. I don't think he was ever bothered by carpetbaggers, in the lost world in those days —we never had them until lately. In fact, there is no record of my grandfather ever taking the oath of Allegiance.

My great-uncle Beverly went down to Mexico City, to serve an Austrian emperor on a hopeless American throne. I believe that there was something about this beautiful gesture of Maximilian's that great-uncle loved more than even that of the Confederacy, and yet, the two gestures were intermingled, confused with each other in the mind of my great-uncle Beverly. In the back of his mind had been the hope, a wild dream that Maximilian might prevail, and that the south would secede again, to unite with Mexico, thereby creating a vast Central American kingdom—ah, but it was a long chance, the essence of never surrender, but it was a dream typical of my great-uncle and quite a few of those desperate adventurers who followed Maximilian down the lonely road to the dust of empire.

The Emperor's star had begun to wane when great-uncle got there, the French under the great Maréschal Bazaine had withdrawn by Napoleon's orders, leaving only the Austrians and Belgians and a division of Legionnaires, and three indifferent Mexican brigades to hold all Mexico. I tell you my great-uncle was crazy. But this seemed to have been the principal fascination, it was Maximilian's devotion *ad absurdum* to a lost cause that appealed to my great-uncle Beverly, late of the most fantastic Lost Cause of them all—he was all in favor of Maximilian and there were no lost causes in this dull world after Maximilian, at least, not for my great-uncle Beverly. He was a faithful follower of the last ruler out of a story book, he was a soldier made to order for this silhouette in the twilight. Great-uncle Beverly had served that eerie empire with fierce loyalty, the sword of destiny hanging over them all to give a fillip to their living. They who served the Emperor were prepared to die, against terrible odds. They were men who seemed never to have been afraid.

It was a sweet and melancholy cause, there was something fine about the Emperor that even the Mexicans loved, but alas, for Maximilian! alas for his poor Empress —they were much too good for Mexico. They had been the unknowing puppets of Napoleon III, foisted on the land by a Foreign Legion that was much too good for Napoleon, mercenaries that Maximilian could not even pay, but who were faithful until the end. Everything but the high heart of the Empire was bankrupt when my great-uncle arrived in Mexico City.

Maximilian was a good man, enlightened and unafraid —that was the trouble. He refused to allow the reforms of Juárez to be abolished by the Church, he was too progressive for the monarchists, he told off Napoleon when he found him out, he adopted the Iturbide child as the Crown Prince of Mexico, he even offered his abdication but the common people wouldn't have it, and then, what else could he do for his adopted country—he gave himself as a martyr to the politicians. And these anointed gentlemen, with the support of the dam Yankees fomenting rebellion, and the Mexican generals whom Bazaine had paroled at Pueblo against his better judgment, these eventually had poor Maximilian shot in the face. But my great-uncle said that the handful of Europeans could have smashed anything in Mexico, if they had been allowed. The Belgians never faltered, nor did the Hungarian Hussars, that white cavalry left waiting in Mexico for a word that never came, while the Emperor went off like a fool to Querétaro with the Mexican brigades, and the bravest of all, ready to serve, the Legion of which great-uncle was the commander, these heroes of a hundred battles were left in Pueblo.

Their hands had been tied by Maximilian, they were not even allowed to rescue their own Emperor! Salm-Salm was the only European officer at the Emperor's side—and great-uncle said something sank in the hearts of the Europeans and their last hopes were shattered, their last hearts were broken, for it is bitter when you are ready to die, to have not even the lost cause to fight for. . . . It was a phantom crown, in a raw backward country, but it was a fair crown, it was fine while it lasted, it was worth the while.

My great-uncle Beverly went into it whole-hearted, it was almost as if he found his spiritual metier in that weird background, he entered into an adventure from which there is no return, he was decorated for bravery with the Order of Guadalupe and made a peer of a realm that was disintegrating, and to show his devotion to the Empress, he married one of her ladies-in-waiting, a princess of the Aztec blood—a gentle, dark creature with great eyes, if we have the right daguerreotype of her.

For my great-uncle Beverly the Empire might have been even the cloth of gold. It is only the lost causes that live, after all. Maximilian is remembered and mourned until this day, but never Juárez. Juárez got justice, Maximilian death, but Maximilian lives. And I think if ever I could believe what I would, if I were allowed to fight for what I chose, to give myself unselfishly, I would fight for a phantom thing, too—why, blood of my blood, great-uncle Beverly, I would fight for the Lost Cause, too!

You were right, you were always right perhaps, there is never anything ridiculous about those who die for the shadow, or those who take the losing side, or those who stand alone, or those in general who live dangerously—because even when you are betrayed, it is with a strange pathos. There was that gentleness to Maximilian, it was some music that he heard in his heart, and he went to fight

Mexicans with Mexicans, he left the bravest of the brave like toy soldiers behind him when he went to defeat and surrender at Querétaro. It was all melodrama, it was perfect—even to the least detail, with a Judas in the form of Colonel López to open the city gates in the dead of night— who committed suicide later in remorse. It can be said of the Mexicans that they all wanted the Emperor to escape, and go back safe to his White Cavalry and his Legionnaires —it was only Juárez who was mean-spirited enough to want the Emperor to die—but this was incompatible with Maximilian's honor, an Emperor does not cut and run, so he had ridden down the hill with Salm-Salm and surrendered to Escobedo, requesting that his native army be paroled and the city of Querétaro spared.

It has all the elements of great drama. Here were men against the gods, and they failed. It ended in humiliation, with the Emperor a prisoner in a dark monastic cell, sick with malaria and dysentery, the brutal soldiery pressing to stare like monkeys at his captivity, at this half-mythical Fair God, who had failed. With a last comic touch—Prince Salm-Salm, indignant that he was not shot at Maximilian's side, insisting on his right as a prince of the blood and a general-of-staff to be executed like Mejía and Miramón!

There was an epilogue, and it was a long time dying— the Empire became a gentle beautiful legend in Mexico, but after the execution there was nothing for the Europeans to do but withdraw, though some of them stayed in the country on parole. Great-uncle Beverly had settled on his wife's estates in Yucatán. He was then a man who had lost three countries, and very embittered about the collapse of the Empire. He could never get over the way the Mexicans shot Maximilian in the face, or that naive man dying with a shout of *Viva Méjico!* They didn't need a Christ in Mexico, great-uncle said, but somebody like Bazaine who wore the pants. It was characteristic of great-uncle Beverly that even though he was in a strange country on good behavior and by the courtesy of his enemies, that he sent challenges to all of Juárez' generals in the field, and in particular Escobedo, the moment he heard that the Empress Carlota had gone mad in Belgium. He sent his challenges to every general in the field, but those bushwhackers all declined the honor, so great-uncle's private war with Mexico died quietly.

I went down there once to look up my folk in Yucatán. I don't know what I expected to find, I guess I expected to arrive at some ante-bellum white house set in live oak festooned with Spanish moss, and that I would find the descendants of my high-minded romantical great-uncle quite grand and a credit to the family. It must be understood, however, that after three generations in Yucatán there was very little English blood left in my distant cousins. I could not tell them from the Mexicans of the better sort, most of them were quite poor, and none of them spoke English. There was quite a tribe of them, called Allende.

They were small planters and tradesmen, better off than the run of their neighbors, although there was no great house in the family or pride that I could see. They lived in *jacales* with thatched roofs and dirt floors and great-uncle Beverly would have found some of his grandchildren illiterate. The elder Allendes remembered him, and as a grand señor in that province, very correct, for they had to kiss his hand when they called upon the old man, and even when they were grown they had treated him with ceremony, or he practically came up out of his easy chair and caned them. He was still spoken of by the ladies in that family as the Conde de la Valle, the title created for great-uncle Beverly by Maximilian, after that given by the King of Spain to Cortés—for the Emperor always said the hawk-faced long-haired Englishman reminded him of a conquistador.

It was too bad that his seed turned out poorly. They were not eagles, and they were not conquistadores, they didn't give a damn about lost causes or sentiment of any kind. Montezuma would never have kept them to breed warriors for his armies. For the grandchildren of great-uncle Beverly had gone to pot as fast as they were able in that climate, and with small grace. They had forgotten their ethos, or they had inherited all the Indian and my great-uncle's weaknesses and none of his virtues. There is a saying that half-breeds never amount to much, they are always fighting themselves.

They were vulgar and indolent people, and most of them treated me insolently, even if I was their cousin and spoke Spanish. Occasionally, I saw the blond hair, and this was most attractive in that dark country, or the merciless blue eyes in a man or woman of the Allendes, and I was reminded of great-uncle Beverly.

9

And now we go back, and we listen to Ernesto Acuña. We can always go back to Ernesto Acuña when the reading is dull. And perhaps we need his raw words, the old times and the bitter beauty as a relief from the frustration and the real ennui of the present, the everlasting mediocrity, the sullen spirituality, the proxy and pornography, the mute inglorious mass suicides of today—at any rate, let us go back for a while to Ernesto Acuña, who lived in a time before the heart of the world was dead. Listen to him, in the drab cantina, look out the door at the white ruins of the walled town of San Juan, and he will tell you about the man who built it.

"Don Juan was a good padrone," Ernesto always said. "He was your last hidalgo, a great robber baron perhaps, but he was a man. He came out of Mexico fighting the French of Maximilian, and it had not been easy to leave the hills of Coahuila, the fiestas and the lands of his father for this bare prairie, this jungle of *monte* and little mountains, this wild horse country unfit for Christians—this insipid land! He hired out fighting the Kiowa Indians, in putting down cattle wars, in recovering stolen cattle. His ranch was a thieves' market, an exchange for stolen herds. He had a way of stealing a man's herd and selling it back to him, cheap. He and his faithful vaqueros, the fathers of Pablo and Andreas and myself and many another, all of them from Coahuila, cheated and plundered until the domain of Don Juan was larger than any north of the river. Don Juan cut out for himself a kingdom. The minstrel will make no apology for that, nor do I. The gringos were grabbing, and so was Don Juan.

"We think Don Juan was a great man, that he brought peace to the border—he subdued the bandits, he made stealing *his* cattle unprofitable, and what if he did kill the Indians, petty landowners, and a few Americanos? It was the times, señor. . . . He was a hidalgo born, he had the right. It would never do to compare him to an outlaw, to some thieving gunman. If anybody had intimated to the old Don that his life had not been upright and honorable, he would have been deeply grieved. He would have felt greatly misjudged, a misunderstood man, and probably would have cut your heart out before he came to his senses. He was a grand old man, and he didn't believe in seeing any side of a question but his own.

"We have listened to him, sitting by our campfires of a night, a wrinkled old man, proud and forbidding and blameless as a king, making his little jest, deploring the past, saying that he had no alternative—the French had taken his lands, what else was there for him? He wasn't going to be without land, he didn't know how to be anything but a hidalgo. It grieved him, he was sorry to take their ranchos, but that was all. Not he, not Don Juan to have a conscience about it, to enjoy taking a man's pasture because the French and Juárez and the good Lord had confiscated his own—those were the things that the good Lord must look after.

"He was censured only by his enemies; or some lurid minstrel, touched with a smoke of marihuana, might tell how the Don had murdered his faithful vaqueros one at a time with his own hands after their service was done, to seal their lips forever. If that were not true, they would argue, what then became of the Old Men, where were their graves? That, ah, I do not know . . . but such tales are fashioned by men who would slander their own mothers.

"There were three-quarter million hectares in Don Juan's kingdom. He built hundreds of miles of brush fence around this pasture, walling himself in with mesquite and gran'hena, his fence riders shooting trespassers like dogs, all travelers who did not come in by the white roads. His was a land of No Trespass. He built his village there on the purple shores of that sunken *laguna,* the most beautiful in the land, fringed with giant huisache trees like green and yellow scattered lace and hemmed in by these stony hills. It was, as you see, in a small valley in a land of little mountains. The streets were cobblestoned or glittering white with *caliche,* and over them here and there were gateways and arches in the style of Guadalajara—I was never in Guadalajara, but that is what men say. The lime-washed buildings were built at the edge of water in a land of little water.

"At the top of the gray and white village, built of adobe and sandstone and *caliche,* overlooking the roads under gaunt arches, the great *laguna* with white houses shadowed in it, the miles of twisted brushland and tiny mountains, was Don Juan's dream of a castle in Coahuila. He always had death in his eyes when he spoke of Coahuila. Perhaps this house was a faithful duplication of one his family had owned; I do not know. It was a great house, it covered the whole of a little mesa. It looked like a rectangular fortress with topless towers, frowning down the unscaleable sides of the cliffs with little ornamentation, few windows. And because of the material which they used, it was hardly finished before it looked crumbling and old as three hundred years.

"Don Juan cast about in his mind for some time for a cattle brand, which is the coat of arms of all great families along the frontier, and a name for his village—something good, something his people could holler and hold on to; and in his cups one day he stamped a bottle of wine upon the table and cried that would be his mark, by Jesús and María, a figure *O,* and long may it reign. And he named his village—it was fifteen years after the place was founded, and the festival was one these dim eyes could never forget—after the saints who had guided him and the ways of his own country, the San Juan, the lovely San Juan on the Baluarte."

Ernesto cleared his throat with a hollow hoarseness and looked about the cantina at the idlers and loftily at a few young men who were singing in falsetto voices. He ordered more to drink, and lowering his voice, he continued—

"Those were the good days, the fair days when we and our fathers built the San Juan. Now, there is something come to pass, it is almost like an enchantment, and we live not well as we did then. There are many strange customs and people and credos come to us from the gringos that we do not understand but which we must welcome and take into our houses because we are Americans. We, too, are Americans, but we can remember San Juan, that belonged to no time and no people and no country.

"Our sons can't, and they are not men who can forefoot wild horses, either. They are nothing like we were, but shiftless and dissolute. Some, grandsons of the old vaqueros who were our fathers, these have gone to school and been trained for clerking in stores and sitting on stools with white collars on, their effeminate hands passing through pomaded hair. And at night they are *chulos* where once their fathers roared and fought for women like so many bulls in a pasture.

"Our daughters have lost their modesty and their shame, they do not arouse men and they are no longer the pride of our hearts or women you'd want children by, but something in those days our people would have stoned from the village. *Ay*, señor, we might have caught these painted jades in the brush afterwards, tracked them down in fact, as men will, but that proves nothing—the truth is that our womenfolk would have stoned the sluts from town.

"Even Little Juan, now that we talk on such a subject, was not a chip from the old block, nor was he particularly like his mother. I have not told how Don Juan came to marry the woman who is the mother of Little Juan. Horses he had in his patio, and his bastards in the village, like any hidalgo, but when he was forty-nine it occurred to the old fellow that he missed something, that he was lonely in the prime of life and needed a woman, a strong woman to be mistress in his house and the mother of his legitimate sons. And none of your civilized canaries for him! He had fought too hard, lived too brutally to have them around, except for ornament—although you would have thought, for a moment, the difficult blood of Castile in his veins, a name which the same viceroys of New Spain had borne, the padrone would have chosen one of the effete ladies of the capital, a Bustamante or Villafranca for his woman.

"But not Don Juan—what he wanted was a vaquera, a woman of the earth, a peasant fearless and passionate, cruel as a witch maybe—something tantalizing and satisfying—and I was with the *corrida* when he found her, in Monterrey. It was after swimming a thousand head of Chihuahuas across the Rio Grande and a long hard drive on a dusty road, and faith, we had been all for a revel. We spent our first night at the Cantina de la Cruz by the walls of the palace of the Bishop. In those days, we were all armed from our enemies, the wine was good, the house and the women were ours. That was as much our country as this between the Nueces and the Rio Grande. We had not a thought but that the fire was warm and the wenches good to look upon. A blue norther had blown us into Monterrey with that great herd of cattle, and the mescal was hot like a coal in the belly.

"We were at peace, at home. But the old Don was not a man to allow another to warm his belly and air his views in the same room with himself, so when the local revelers pushed in the door, being brave with tequila or mescal, there was nothing left but to shoot them out again. What with the screaming of wenches and the lamps falling riddled and the oil flaming up in one corner of the ballroom and Andreas hollering like a baby that somebody had stuck his ear to the wall with a dagger, it was all a rotten mess. Nobody was hurt, but it *sounded* terrible. The old

Don winged a man as he took a leap through the door into the moonlight and I heard the coyote screams of one or two others who might have been stung by a bullet in the dark, but they were all running down the crooked alleys not yet out of wind—this is beside the point; as a fracas, it was not interesting, but I am telling you about it because then and there was when the old Don fell in love. I suppose you would call it love, even a hidalgo can fall in love.

"We were not aware of this woman Marina until the intruders were gone and we were stumbling around in the darkness. All the rest of the sluts had fled with the fat madame, holding up their petticoats and quacking like geese. This one was etched against the flames in the corner, doing her best to keep the house from burning down, I don't know why. It was a living, and she wasn't going to be done out of it, she might even have liked that house. She was smothering the flames as quickly as they sprouted with serapes and jackets, ponchos and sombreros and anything of ours she could lay hands on, meanwhile cursing us in a manner that made us shout with admiration. Every once in a while, she would get out a good one, and we would shout in admiration.

"Any fool in the dark could tell as she stood against the flames, that she had a leg on her. Every movement she made was *puro bruto*. The hair fell down about her eyes and she would swing the sweat off with her hand like a woman in the corn-fields. The color of the fire leaping all over her body in rich dark red and shadow, caressing it like silk, made a pretty picture. The old Don muttered hoarsely as much, and demanded her brought to him instantly.

"She lived in that house, but *por Dios!* you would have thought her a queen the way she acted, like no man had ever touched her before—she needed gentling. It took three vaqueros to drag this woman squawking and kicking to Don Juan, and then they looked like they had been scratched by black-brush; one of them was cut across the nose with a dagger and would have been murdered if he had not grabbed and shaken it out of her hand like a man shakes off a snake. She stood there before the old Don, indignant and trying to get her breath, but as soon as she did, Marina smiled.

"It is hard to describe Marina as she was in those days; although she still lives, señor, with her hair gray as a she-goat's and her teeth all gone. She had the smiling eyes that all men love; they could be like stars, and then, they could be like stone in a Toltec idol's eyes. Her lips were soft and sweet and not hard like the firm bitter beauty of her body. Her body was beautiful, as if it had been swept by the wind and rain in the yellow moons, and her lips were lovely as those fixed in a picture, or death. She did not step or go wobbling like other women, but she strode easily with the light collected tread of a fine mare.

"And for splendor and wonder and pomp, in all this world no one has been married like Marina—what a festival we had at the San Juan! It was the same as the end of a three years' drought, even better. Don Juan had us dressed in buckskin and lace and the very trappings of our horses encrusted with gold and silver. The music was both by night and day, until the ragged minstrels fell faint from singing. While the streets of San Juan were crowded with people from everywhere and the gayest colors, the bravest

costumes the land has ever seen. I can remember it all plain as yesterday.

"In the afternoon when the sun had cooled, we held our rodeos in the great clearing by the moat-lake before the eyes of Don Juan and his bride. We tailed the bull, roped wild cattle and rode the wildest horses that could be had from El Paso to San Luis Potosí. And there were musicians, the very best from Monterrey. There was a circus in the street, and real gypsies. It must have cost thousands of pesos, but Don Juan was not the man to stint; there was celebration for all the ladies in their finery, and sport enough for men, with meat and grog at any hour of the day or night in the halls of the great house, and no murder done, no brawling at all out of respect to Don Juan and his madonna.

"Their wedding was no such thing as a fiesta of ours, señor. Don't you judge them by the likes of us you have seen in this sorry land. There was no raucous insult and incidental murder, or crazed drunk peon girl to be dragged kicking from the rank brawl to the house of her vaquero. There was no screaming of women as the family left her in tears, putting ashes on their heads, the poor groom making awkward, embarrassed appeals to quiet the bride. Jesús, how they screamed—I remember mine! And we were rough men to be touched by the wonder of them, so we'd cuff their ears until they let up, the racket they made was unbearable, and after that they were gentler. It was routine, you might say. But Don Juan's woman was not such a one. She must have had blood in her somewhere.

"There was no following *her* husband like a *soldadera*, or aborting in line camps, for this woman of Don Juan's—

no shamefaced clumsy circle of brush riders was outside when she gave birth to Little Juan. There was no burying of stillborn children in the cowlot, like we do them—no shoveling the dirt in their faces and having done with it, but Marina had a coffin and priest and flowers and things when Little Juan's sister was born dead two years later. This alone shows that she had caste. I suppose it was all right in its way, but it's strange to us that you must bury someone who has never been *alive,* and pay the padre for candles. But Don Juan and his wife were *buena gente,* and not to be marveled at by the like of us.

"Those were the good days, señor, the good rich days, when we left our village in the dim of dawn thereafter with always for the years to come a bit of sash or tatter of lace to remember them by! We didn't ask for much, only for a padrone and the white village and enough to eat. Our horses stepped high and threw their heads, bridled with silver bits, and we sang in the morning as we followed the long dead river of the Baluarte. We tracked cattle through the *mogotes,* we broke the young horses, and we raided into Mexico at a word from the padrone when things were dull. And when the work was done of an evening, or we were returned perhaps from many miles of journey, we would ride under the great walls of Don Juan's castle, passing jests and salutations and *gritos* with him, somehow dauntlessly and good-naturedly, so that he would turn from the balcony and smile upon his young wife with content."

10

AND THERE WERE stories Javier used to tell around the campfires, with a large wealth of detail and his own peculiar humor. The two traits principally misunderstood in the Mexican are his hard head and his sense of humor. The Mexican children are born with rocks in their hands. And I once thought the vaqueros humorless, solemn and pig-eyed and fierce, a little monstrous, but now that I look back on their humor it seems to have salt and gusto in our pallid times.

Javier was always a humorist, he kept the vaqueros laughing. I seem to remember those vaqueros always laughing, they were young and wiry and cruel. They shouted through the brush like maniacs during the day, but at night in the black dark they were quiet, holding herd, and I remember their muted voices and the songs they sang. They seemed always to be riding into dim dawns that were somehow hushed like the moment before revelation—into that darkness that came down over Egypt —into that terrible *monte* of the lost world, in single file, stealthily so as not to scare the ladinos and then they flushed them, they went shouting through the brush as the ladinos broke it down—it was a fine life, a fine time and they laughed and they sang and they lived dangerously.

They were rather exquisite young men, like cavaliers. And even when there was little time before the crucial daybreak, and we were all impatient like soldiers waiting for the signal to attack, I remember Chávez was softspoken and courteous with the *compañeros,* as he called them—even ceremonious, polite, correct is the word, like the master of a ship at sea. He always had time for courtesy, and he believed in dignity like all illiterate people, and with this in mind he would address the companions: "Will you do me the favor of taking that *mogote,* young Rafael? If you please, Don Miguel, with my friend Juanito, will you sweep the cattle through the north canyon? All of you, señores, we shall rendezvous at Agua Dulce." Nobody ever thought of calling Chávez by any except his last name.

I could never understand the waste of ceremony and this grandiloquence, for I would ask in my youthful ignorance, if he was foreman and these men were being paid to obey him, why should he be so unfailingly polite, it was an extravagance with precious time, and upon hearing this Javier, who was the *corrida*-boss and always rode behind us, would laugh and say, you can lead the Mexicans, padrone, but you can never force them. And it is just as our young padrone has learned, we are *valientes* upon occasion, although Esteban will have it like an old woman that we are brave only to eat—the fact is, that every Mexican born of woman is stubborn as a mule. A little humor will go a long ways, and courtesy. Yes, my young friend shall learn this thing, and by his leave—for Javier liked me, and he wanted always to be correct with those he liked —the young padrone shall see, he shall know that every vaquero being Mexican, has the head of a burro.

Javier was a man past middle age then, robust in the prime of life, with an open manner and a moon-like face, pig eyes with wrinkles at the corners, a cruel smiling mouth, and no beard—he was perhaps half-Yaqui and had been born in Sonora. What was most interesting about him was that for many years he had been in the army of Pancho Villa. All the *charros* of Sonora and Coahuila had ridden with Pancho Villa to liberate the people, even as their fathers had been *rurales* with Porfirio Díaz, but in that case, only because there was a great glory to good cavalry. Javier was another who had much to say around the campfire at night, when he did not have to listen respectfully to the Old Men, and his stories were spicy like fresh venison seasoned with *chiltipiquin*.

He kept the vaqueros laughing, sometimes he could not continue, they roared and made such a noise. Particularly at the bull-in-the-china-shop antics of Fierro the Butcher, and some of the stories told about this right hand of Pancho Villa were as good as those of Paul Bunyan. I laughed as much as the vaqueros did, because after all, I was raised among them.

He told his stories in a voice that was light with mockery, for in this bulk of a man there was no depth of utterance, and some of the men were sly behind his back and said with all that fat, that Javier was a *castrado*, but he just had the high shrill voice of most plains people. He was a clown unconsciously, like Luro, and because of this Chávez wisely kept him in charge of the men, for Chávez told me it was ever thus with the Mexicans, that whenever you saw one doing all the talking, at whom the men laughed most, you had either to fire him because he spoiled their heads that were notional as those of burros, or you made the big talker *corrida*-boss.

And asking if these tales that Javier told were true about Pancho Villa, Chávez said they were—and he reminded me of a raid I had witnessed in the Randado country when I was eight years old. Forty of the Villista cavalry had come sixty miles in from Rio Grande to steal horses, and I remember how the vaqueros fortified themselves in the brush corrals that were like barricades, but the Dorados or whatever they called themselves at the time had not fired a shot at us, they had ridden past as if they did not intend to molest anyone or anything on the Jesús María, because we had always been friends with the Mexicans, passing jests and salutations with the vaqueros, with many of whom they were acquainted and even related, and I remember their saddlery *was* glittering with rosettes of silver and they wore ornaments that looked like gold. "And do you know who was in charge of that outfit?" Chávez asked. "It was none but your *compadre* Javier, who is now *corrida*-boss of the Jesús María, even reformed. Of course, that was during the revolution, and it never reflects on Javier's honesty. But at the time, the Villistas had come back during the night and all but robbed us of every horse on the ranch."

"We were called Dorados," Javier explained around the campfire, "because our saddles were covered with golden rosettes, and our bridles trimmed with gold, our spurs and pistol butts and knife handles plated with it, because we couldn't take it with us and the Dorados didn't live forever. We comprised the bodyguard of Pancho Villa himself, and we were a good cavalry. That was back when men used cavalry, and war was fun. The Golden Ones, they called us, and we were young, then," Javier said. "That was a long time ago."

"Fierro was our General, a good companion, but very brutal. He used to kill Obregón's men with his bare hands, and he was strong as a horse. He shot all the sentries who slept at their posts, muttering, *'Pobrecito! Pobrecito!'* when he did, for he was not a man without sentiment. When he took a town he sometimes tied the Chinese together by their pigtails and burned them alive, because he hated Chinamen, and he would not have you consider him a man without humor. He was good to his Dorados, though; he loved us like brothers. We were his sort of *gente,* we followed wherever he led us, even if it was to rope the yanquis behind machine guns, and a great many of us were killed. Obregón used yanquis behind machine guns, and big Negroes like Ben for officers —but then, we had a yanqui aviator, and Reilly. But I want to tell you how strong Fierro was, and it makes this little story.

"There was a time when Fierro lay in hiding, having had a horse shot from under him in a night raid, but learning that Pancho Villa with six hundred Dorados was to attack the town of Muzquiz, our General made haste to steal another horse and join his commander, although he arrived too late to take part in the battle. He was but a few miles off when he saw three of our horsemen riding at a furious gallop, bearing news of the defeat of Obregón by the glorious arms of Pancho Villa, and Fierro hailed them, while the principal messenger, recognizing in Fierro the man they were looking for, jumped down from his horse, and coming to a sort of military salute, he exclaimed:

" 'Good news, my General, good news, my General! Long live the Revolution! The Federals are conquered, and their asses are dragging from every lamp-post in the town!'

"And so great was the joy of Fierro at these glad tidings, that he too dismounted and threw himself upon the trooper, giving many *gritos,* long-lives to Pancho Villa, vivas for the Revolution, and like a man, ending with the *abrazo,* saying, 'Embrace me, *compañero!* Embrace me, my brave!' but such a stretch was that, and so strong was the embrace of my *compadre* Fierro that the soldier gave one cry, '*Ay!*' and fell doubled at his feet, mouthing a torrent of blood. Fierro had been a little embarrassed—he who in hand-to-hand fighting used to kill not with the pistol or machete but with his hands, rolling up his sleeves with gusto and hugging men to death like a bear—he had forgotten in his enthusiasm how strong he was. And this soldier happening to be one of Fierro's own, the other officers trumped up a pleasantry, for an inquiry was held.

"Pancho Villa absolved his General of all blame, of course, because Fierro in this case had been an involuntary murderer, and Pancho Villa had a large genial way of looking on misdemeanors of this sort, but he positively prohibited in the future, under pain of death, that his General Fierro, his own right hand and his brother in the Dorados—and how it hurt Don Pancho to issue such an order, we can never know—embrace *anyone, friend or enemy, woman or child*. I was a sentinel at Headquarters that day," Javier said, "and I remember Fierro stood at attention with the sweat beading his face that looked like the relief maps on the walls, and he took this injunction very seriously. It was even said that this depriving our General of his right to embrace embittered Fierro, he was such a sensitive man, and that was the reason he was uncongenial, and why he burnt the Chinamen, until that too was forbidden him, and shot all the dogs in the plaza, for he had a big heart and he wanted to enjoy himself when he took a town, and it was very tame to just shoot civilians.

"And another time, I remember," and Arturo smiled as if he were enjoying a huge joke with himself, "I was with Fierro and his Dorados outside the city of Chihuahua. It was the middle of October, and we had besieged and shelled that town since the dog-days, and were fed-up. But one night we entered by stealth, and the next morning found the citizens of Chihuahua in a fix, for when they had risen to open the windows and doors to let in the free grace of God, they looked out and they found Fierro all unexpected with fifty of his Dorados, and these had put in prison various principal men of the town and had hung, not willy-nilly a pair of poor devils, but the Mayor and the Governor of the State, first citizens of Chihuahua and mind you, men good enough to ransom.

"Furthermore, Fierro with his Dorados sitting easily in the saddle, was predicting sweetly to the people in the plaza that if they did not accept Don Pancho Villa as their president at once, who was waiting outside the city with the bulk of his army, that he was resolved to keep on hanging and he would put the town to sack. At this the council speedily convened. It was composed at that time of the licentiates Cepeda, Tejada and Santos as the fourth member had fled, declaring he wanted nothing to do with Pancho Villa. And the other three, frightened with the menace of Fierro in the main plaza, discussed the point in question lightly, not having time for large discourse or flowery rhetoric with Fierro roaring outside the window and the Dorados sitting in their saddles with their fangs bared, and made an act recognizing the Revolution and Don Pancho Villa as the new President of Mexico. Yet, when it came time for this Santos to sign, who was nothing but an old cuttlefish," Arturo said, "he looked out at the Dorados slouching in their saddles and he began to write a cross and underneath it, before he scrawled his name, he wrote: 'I attest before God and this ✠ and the words of the Evangelists that I sign out of three motives— for fear, from fear, and of fear.'

"This our General could not read, being illiterate, but he wanted everything legal, so he had Reilly the yanqui who was one of our Captains read it, and upon hearing this tribute to himself and his Dorados, Fierro was vastly amused, and clapped old Santos on the back so that the old man fell flat on his face to the floor. Fierro laughed, and Reilly who was by no means a lawyer assuring him it was strictly legal, we can get on with the story. Which is, that this licentiate Santos even if he was an old cuttlefish, lived in the company of a daughter, Teresa by name, a girl pretty from head to foot, seventeen years old and who had in her veins enough of humanity and Castile for one to conjecture that virginity was not pleasing to her.

"Soon Teresa, as is natural with a young girl, was to have a beau and he was none other than this same Reilly, who was more or less commandant for Fierro, and somehow contrived to get married in every town that we had taken. He was a nice-appearing young man with red hair, and when Fierro was sentimental he said that Reilly was his right hand, his son, and because of this prestige, Reilly was safe from assassins in the army who might have objected to gringos. All that Reilly had to fear was Fierro himself, who was something formidable, for he would sometimes get drunk, and he could not tell his right hand from his left in that condition, but blithely he would shoot first and then say he was sorry. It was all a mistake. If it happened to be a friend, he would even cry a little. Of course, Reilly had been refused by the girl's father, for Santos came of a proud old family, and our gallant was much discouraged, and put his suit before the General, who that day was sitting in state in a cantina by the square that is called the Alma de Méjico.

" 'What does he mean!' yelled the furious Fierro, as the rest of us lounged at the bar, witnessing this little comedy but gravely polite—enjoying ourselves with mescal *del gallo,* the very best, and all the sluts in Chihuahua to content us, and outside we knew our horses were fat and our saddles ornamented with gold that no man dared steal—it was a good time for us, señor," Arturo said. "Our General veered around in the chair, and looked incredulously at Reilly. 'What!' he shouted again. 'A masquerade of a licentiate to refuse my commandant, who is a pearl among youths, indeed he is! *Seguro que sí!* I shall myself talk with the old father. Let us go, you rogue—don't be confounded, for I am, or I am not Francisco de Fierro, your General and the right hand of Pancho Villa, but you shall be married this morning. And I your best man, using the name my own mother baptized me with. . . . And all these gentlemen of gold shall be ushers, or I shall know the reason why,' he added, glaring at us along the bar, and we squirmed.

" 'It grieves me though, my son Reilly, that you are really in love, again. Because you must know by now, my lad, that love is the wine that quickest changes to vinegar; but that is no care of mine, but yours. What I have to do is get you married, and then between you and your Teresa you can multiply until you are worn out. Personally though, I don't see why you insist on marrying all these young women—it is so unnecessary, all you have to do is to say the word, and you know that I would have a requisition written out for her. You could write it yourself.'

"But Reilly was a fine Catholic, he even crossed himself in battle, and he would not think of taking a girl without the sanction of the padre. So in this instance our fine old cavalryman of Pancho Villa heaved his bulk out of a chair, knocked a few bottles and glasses clattering to the floor, adjusted his two cross-belts on his chest like a bull's, his two cartridge belts on his hips and the revolvers in their holsters, and tipping his sombrero in his eyes he stalked with much clinking of spurs down the street to the house of the judge, and without wasting words he got the daughter's hand for his commandant Reilly. The poor Santos had been greatly mortified, bubbling a thousand excuses, as who would not to that formidable bandit, and ended by giving his consent. But when the notary asked that he inscribe this consent and Reilly insisted, who wanted a pure conscience in these matters, the old man sighed, and taking the goose quill in hand, wrote: 'I contest by this ✠ that I consent out of three motives—for fear, from fear, and of fear.'

"Which is as good," Javier claims, "as the ninety and nine reasons alleged by our artilleryman why he had not fired a shot in the capture of Durango: 'The first reason was, I had no powder,' that man said, for he was an Englishman and he had no sense of humor, 'and the other ninety-eight, I keep to myself.' Anyway, that was the manner in which the three motives of the licentiate became a phrase with the soldiers of Pancho Villa, and we moved eventually to the south of Chihuahua, we went all the way to Mexico City, but Reilly made the licentiate's daughter a good husband, as good a husband as she could have wanted, for a little while.

"Those were great days, señor. We had a lot of laughs in those days," Javier said.

11

THE CRUELLEST TALE that Javier ever told was the one of the time when Fierro and his Dorados raided this ranch in Hidalgo County, to avenge a mistreatment by Don Santiago of Javier himself a long time before, when Javier was a horsebreaker on that ranch. They had called Fierro the Little Blood in those days, and he had gone on the raid in person, and this is the story of Javier's revenge on Don Santiago.

It is also a footnote to their Mexican morality. Most of the folk in Hidalgo were humble rancheros, but there had been this one family, the de la Torres, with pretensions. They owned fifty miles of brush and river-bottom along the Rio Grande, twelve miles deep in *porciones*. Their hacienda that now lies in ruins stood on a hill, and it was like a small walled town overlooking that flat empty land. They were good people, gentry—good as any in

Laredo and rich—Don Santiago de la Torre and his brother Humberto and Don Santiago's son, Antonio.

Mexico had been hell-broken-loose for years, rebellion was chronic and devastating, and there were raids into the Rio Grande valley, even as far north as Randado. They were instigated by Villa, led by men like the Little Blood. At that time the Little Blood was a younger man, without the dreadful reputation he later earned as the right hand of Pancho Villa. My friend Javier was one of the Little Blood's lieutenants, and he remembers his chief with regard. He says that the Little Blood was quite a presentable young man, slight and a bit fastidious, with a black mustache.

All of Tamaulipas had been sacked by his cavalry. There was not a rich man to be ransomed or a horse to be stolen from Monterrey to Matamoras to Nuevo Laredo. But the Little Blood was of enterprising spirit, and herding his ragamuffin cavalry into the Rio Grande—at that time these cavalrymen were not prosperous or called the Golden Ones, except in fun—he paid Don Santiago a visit, after hearing glowing accounts from Javier of the old man's wealth and pride. The Little Blood couldn't stand pride. And great was his wrath when he found that all the horses had been scattered into the brush, that the Revolution had been betrayed, and that Don Santiago, a man of thrifty, even mean habit, kept no gold or silver on the place.

The Little Blood was hurt, outraged, ashamed for the hidalgo. This was no way for an hidalgo to be! He ordered them all, man, woman and child into the courtyard —every cowherd and laborer, all the servants no matter how humble, the dignified miserly padrone and his protesting gray-haired shrew of a wife, Don Humberto and the woman he lived with, called Guadalupe, who was not yet thirty and passing fair—Javier was to have her for himself—and Antonio who was practically a bridegroom, having just been married to a beautiful girl from San Luis Potosí.

The rebel chief had them herded into the walled enclosure like cattle, while his men sat in their saddles, fingering their carbines or looking in their silver pommel mirrors to straighten their attire—for even then they were preparing to be the famous Dorados, and were vain as girls. The family stood a little above the horsemen, on a veranda, and the servants and laborers huddled together like sheep at the base of the steps. The Little Blood held the reins of his horse, he made them an elegant bow and a little speech, and he ended thus:

"And since you dogs and gringos have run the horses off, and have no valuables, I will give certain of you a chance to live, and shoot the rest." The Little Blood smiled then. "All you women that want your men to live, step forward. You shall sleep with my Dorados, and have something to brag about—and your men shall live."

Fierro enjoyed the anticlimax in those days, Javier said. It was before he became coarse and drunken and jaded. He could have shot the men, and taken the women—they were at his mercy, anyway—or if he had wanted to indulge his indignation over Don Santiago's shameless frugality, and this is what hurt the Little Blood most, he could have tortured them all. He had with him a Maya from Zapata's army who was a past master at torture. But in that day Fierro, alias the Little Blood, was subtle.

"You step out front, and you sleep with my Dorados."

The people of the hacienda looked back into the eyes of the Dorados, brave and fanatical young men, and swallowed the insult. Not a soul among the laborers or herdsmen or the servants or the family stirred. The women looked with fear and flashing eyes at the bandits, and the men of the great hacienda dared not look their contempt, dropping their eyes and spitting on the ground softly. Not hard enough to offend the Little Blood, understand—he might have been something of an exquisite, but the Little Blood had cold eyes, and when he smiled, it made them afraid. His Dorados were ragged and a little ridiculous, they covered their saddlery with ornaments, and wore their hair long like Indians, but they were without mercy and without fear. So the men of the hacienda said not a word, but every one of them, including Don Santiago and Humberto and Antonio, stepped in front of their women and stood ready.

"And is that all?" asked the Little Blood, smiling, and looking them over as if they were very poor cattle indeed. "And is that all?" he asked again, dismayed. "Very well, *muy bien*," he added calmly.

He commanded his Dorados to herd the men to the adobe wall that made a fortress of this hacienda he had taken by surprise, and every man was stood against the wall. And all the boys, because the Little Blood could not stand to have enemies, and Mexican children grow up so vindictively. The women began to weep, especially the peon women, the lowborn ones, but none of them made a move. Except Antonio's wife, the proudest woman on the place. She was beautiful even with the tears in her eyes, she was young and lovely as a song. She was so

beautiful, Javier said it made you catch your breath and marvel.

She gave a great cry and ran to the bandit chief, "I will! I will! Anything . . ." she cried, "but spare my Antonio, spare the husband of my heart, *por Dios!* Señor, I beg of you!"

She was the only one of the women, highborn or low, to make the plea, and she ran to him and begged the cruel Little Blood for the life of her husband whom she loved better than honor. And talking to the Little Blood was useless, she was less than dirt to him.

Antonio did not look at her. He stood proudly with his father and uncle looking straight ahead. The women behind Antonio's wife suddenly became silent, while the children looked on quite calmly, with big eyes. The men lined against the wall did not look up for shame. Today, we don't even know her name, the name of that brave woman! Her name lies buried in disgust, and no man mentions the name of that brave woman.

The Little Blood had smiled wickedly, Javier said. He smiled and fingered his mustache while the young wife sank to her knees in front of him and begged for Antonio's life. The bandit knew that later he would do with her as he pleased. Javier said he eventually turned her over to his vilest men. He could have tortured the hacienda folk for rare entertainment, he hated them all, but at the time the idea did not amuse him. He twirled his mustache and looked down on this lovely creature from San Luis Potosí, listening to her entreaties, and waiting for Antonio to crack.

Her pleading was as music to the young bandit's ear. He noticed that Antonio was pale, white as a gringo in fact, but that he stood with his head in the air, proudly. Then, the Little Blood ordered a firing-squad out of their saddles. Antonio still would not speak, nor make a sign—until his wife begged the bandit for the last time, the tears running down her beautiful face. She had a face like a flower. The Little Blood noticed how white and lovely was her throat, and how the cross of gold on the breasts was piquant, and perhaps he remembered the throat of that gringo whore he had cut in Juárez, and he smiled as she sank on the ground sobbing, and her dress settled in the dust like the discarded cape of a matador. Only the movement of her grief fluttered the shoulders under the garment. Her head was buried in the dirt, and she was saying, *"Ay, por Dios, señor!"* She was crying, *"Ay, por Dios . . ."*

The *pobrecito,* Javier would mutter, and say; it was only then that there had been tears in Antonio's eyes, but they were tears of rage and shame. He was a man—a *gauchipin,* and Javier hated the guts of that entire family —yes, but Antonio was a man! And he spoke for the first time, and he shouted as the fusillade rang out, and the bullets buried in the soft bodies and *caliche* walls, "You slut . . . you dirty slut!"

The Little Blood had smiled. He never could endure the *gauchipins,* Javier said. It was a long time ago—but the bullet holes are still in the crumbling wall.

12

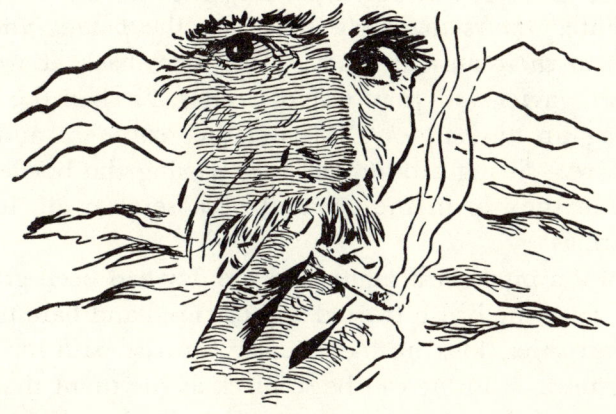

WE HAD A WEIRD STORY told to us by a dope addict around the campfire at Agua Dulce one Christmas Day. Perhaps we were the sort of men who attracted weird and violent tales, but the fact remains, if you told us a story it had to be good. We lived in a raw land, and we wanted salt in our entertainment. They say that he who has smoked the marihuana feels twice-intense, the limbs of his beloved are monstrous, frijole and tortillas comprise a feast, and the taste of plain mescal is as nectar—that's what they say, smoking marihuana is something I've never tried. I've always found life interesting enough without it, but they do say the dreams are splendid, that marihuana gives the mind an intensely clear, or if it is desired, an amassingly turbulent and volcanic cast, peace like that derived from eating the lotus, or a madness the addicts say is divine.

This minstrel, one of those grotesques that are awry

and jangled from smoking this humble weed, stumbled out of the brush that night and into the light of our campfire abruptly. It was Christmas Day but the Mexicans had celebrated theirs the night before at the *posada* and by going to their annual Mass, so we were back at work—Chávez, Javier and Juan Calvos *crudos,* Esteban the cook beating up his *panoches,* Miguel the *remudero* and old Guiterrez—sitting around the fire, passing the bottle, because of the nip in the air, and because after all, it was Christmas.

It was a pitch-dark night, and the day had been gray as a fog, with the brush twisted and tortured and bare under overcast skies, looking like a crazy futurist painting of a wilderness. Nothing can be so black as the night that follows such an ominous day, and it seemed we had such nights all that winter, depressing nights, nights that were almost dreadful. This man lurched out of the black night into the spot where our fire licked furtively against the disheartening dark, and so suddenly he startled us, we were on our feet in astonishment, and had rifles in our hands.

We didn't know at first if he were a *tequilero* or a *mojado* or some tramp from Pena. Then we relaxed, and we laughed out loud, it was only this Calistro of a minstrel. He was a ragged little man with a guitar, like the grasshopper in the fable. His lower lip hung loosely like Calistro's, he drooled and mumbled in his beard, he came to the campfire shuffling in sandals wrapped in hemp, he warmed his backsides diffidently, he ate like a glutton of the jerked beef and rice, praising old Esteban to the skies —and that alone took a *boca-de-ora*—and then he sat down to sing for his supper. This is the tale he told, and he was an intelligent man.

"There was a city in the Sierra Madres, west of Torreón," he said. "I do not know if that is the name of those mountains, but it is what they were called in Coahuila, they are so large and so steep and the ascent so hazardous that they seem to be the mother range of all the mountains. This city was two thousand years old, and it was a dead city—but once it had been the capital of the Toltec empire which ruled the Western World and whose people worshiped the Serpent of the Moon. I know, because I was there, I saw all these things with my own eyes.

"I was a young man, señores—ah, and how often we Old Men use that phrase—when the good things of life happen to you. I had got in a scrape over a girl in the village of Malpais, where I had been playing on my guitar at a fiesta, and I killed a man—young men are always sticking knives in other young men—and I fled to the mountains, but his kinsmen were after me, they followed close on my heels, and I went farther in those mountains than anyone had ever been. I went so far the kinsmen did not dare to follow.

"Those mountains were high in the heavens, and it was cold as the north country. I was a fugitive, ragged and tattered and afraid, tempted to turn back. I could look down on the dusty plain of Torreón, and it was dear, I could see the fields like patches in a quilt, and the glittering white villages warm and lovely, but of a sudden they faded completely from sight and then I saw only the mist and the mountain, and all that I heard was a terrible *hush! hush!* The trees were stunted and twisted like the sketches of Goya. I passed the snowline, and I reached the summit of this particular mountain, but I could not see down the Other Side.

"At first I could not see down the Other Side. It was like groping in a fog, but I went down into that wilderness that had never been penetrated—the good citizens of Torreón say that the Sierra Madres have no Other Side, just a beginning and no end, that they are there like Time and Space—but I descended the Other Side because being a man of some education, I was more afraid of the kinsmen than the Unknown. And I never regret it—for I stumbled down this mother of a mountain until I saw that city of the Toltecs three thousand feet below, when at last I penetrated the blanket of that mist, and it was in a pocket, a basin like a cup, fenced, walled in by these intolerable mountains that reach to heaven, incomparable, and at last, in the sunlight!

"It had been raining in these wind-swept sodden mountains, the rain came down in sheets or in a deluge like a curtain at the opera billowing on a stage—the same curtain of rain that some of you might have seen on a tropical coast, but this was luminous rain, eerie rain. You passed through that rain and came out on the Other Side, and it was to enter another world. I suddenly passed an imaginary boundary, do you understand, a limit set by the realities that men believe, and there I was—out of time, out of mind. You must not think such a thing is strange, for once I was a student of philosophy and we often debated the possibilities of such a marvel.

"And I can't explain it to you, señores, but all of my life, and part of it was spent on the beach at Vera Cruz where the rain comes down pitilessly, I had dreamed of penetrating the curtain of that mysterious rain. It was my destiny, do you understand, I dreamt of it, this was my illusion. I had expected to find beyond the rain a world marvelous, one such as St. Augustine described in his *City of God*. Or that I should find the Fountain of Gold the poor deluded Ponce de Léon searched for in Florida, or that I should find mythical and extravagant treasure like the conquistadores. For you must know that in those days I was a young man and highly fanciful; I used to write flowery verse in the manner of Amado Nervo, of what I would some day find behind the Curtain of Rain. It was a Curtain of Rain with me, señores, *that* was the illusion of my youth. What if I did penetrate it, by chance—what if I did find my illusion, fleeing the vengeance of a dead man's kin—I can see you are not inclined to believe me at all, but this was really vouchsafed me, and when I was challenged by Illusion, when I went into that Unknown, the very gods protected me. *I have amused the gods, señores.* There was something unearthly in the way the rain fell in those terrible mountains, it had been a veritable screen hiding the secrets of God—but why do I tell you these things, when you do not believe?

"I might have been ill at the time, I concede you that. I was drained of courage and strength, and starved and in stress, for crossing those mountains it had been cold and desolate as when Bolívar crossed the Andes. You could not breathe, those mountains were so high. But I had passed the ultimate curtain of the icy rain, and the mist cleared, and I looked down on a city of palaces more beautiful than Mexico, white in the sunlight, a strange benign sunlight that did not look real after my hardship—it was a false illumination, utterly weird, like the gleam from a tomb. And as I stood three thousand feet or more above this incredible city, it seemed a dream, a mirage like the Cities of Cíbola—something the old conquistadores might have seen and described and forgotten in their ignorant way, because nobody would believe them. But I was a scholar, I had studied for the priesthood, and I will swear by the Mother of God, señores, and you must believe me —I saw just such a city as the conquistadores had seen, poor devils—and I was to forget its location the same as they did, because nobody believed me, either.

"It is part of the spell that an enchanted city casts, you look at it and you are turned to pillars of salt, and you forget it, and it was ever merciful thus, or men had been driven mad by forbidden and remembered beauty like I have seen, or they would waste their lives in futile searching for enchanted cities they would never find. I am not one to laugh at the old narrations of conquistadores, or to think them foolish or deranged by hardship and hunger and thirst, because these were hard-headed men, looking for gold. And I have entered a forbidden city, I went through its gates, I walked in its streets—I know. I speak of the things I know.

"I entered the town over a causeway, for like the City of Mexico in the old times it had been surrounded by water, a placid water on all sides—there were fishing boats and outrigger canoes on it, but they seemed to be stuck like paper-boats frozen in glass. And I came to the high walls, the white walls where these hawk-nosed sentinels stood, beserker red devils, six feet tall, gorgeous in raiment of feathers and fine mantles—but they looked straight ahead, and they did not see me as I sneaked past their silent and majestic challenge, greatly dreading. They were under some spell, as if a sudden plague had struck them unawares, or they seemed asleep like the guardians of a castle in Perrault's fairy tales. That is the only way I can describe them, they were out of a story I heard when I was a little boy. They were frozen like the sentinels that Charles of Sweden left behind him in the snow. They were resigned in death like the sad Roman soldiers at Pompeii. They were like men who had been stricken by a death that you can breathe.

"I can't describe the uncanny feeling they gave me, I had an idea they were alive. They were wild haired and fierce and splendid, and I sneaked past them like a beggar, I can tell you, for I could not help but feel that I was committing some dreadful trespass or even a sacrilege. I had a stronger fear that I was alone in that populous city, and that these sentinels would suddenly come awake and cry alarm, until the entire populace of beserkers and Toltecs and these living dead would come swarming down upon me. I had visions of the terrible sacrifice they would make of me to their serpent gods. For there were designs of serpents everywhere, scrawled high on the terraced buildings like tabus, or crawling like Chinese dragons in bas-relief along the foundations. *No, I was not a dauntless magician come to undo a weird enchantment, or awaken a princess from her long sleep—I sneaked into that great town like a thief, like a homeless dog with its tail between its legs.*

"The streets were golden, or at least the cobble was flecked with gold. There were precious stones above each door like amulets, rubies and rare obsidian and jade that the Toltecs prized highly, while all the houses were white with plaster. The domes of the temples were of what seemed a burnished metal, glittering in that eerie sunlight, that sunlight made expressly for this city. They tell you lies who say the Toltecs did not know how to fashion a roof into a dome, for I have seen these temples with my own eyes, and they were splendid and oriental as anything in the books of India.

"Around the temples there were sacred areas, but the rest of the city was disordered, a confusion of houses crowded on every street, thrown together like the cotes of any European city. I remember it reminded me of Córdoba. Houses stacked and scattered like discards, misshapen design and awry enclosures. It was a city in a crazy dream and shadow, once you got into it. But from a distance it was a city seen from the sea, or one you could imagine broadcast in the *barrancas,* or such as might rise from the ice and snow in the north country. It was a shimmering cubistic city, fair to see in that unearthly light. A city of white slums, once you were in it, and with yet the magnificent spires and angles, vaulted roofs without buttresses, shining like gold, and in the sacred areas were temples massive as Notre Dame.

"You must remember, señores, that I have education, that I come of *buena gente*—though I am a tramp, a minstrel and a clown for your amusement, I was educated at Salamanca, and I traveled in France and Spain and Italy, and I come of good family. It was the wine that I drank when I was young, it was the false hilarity that fascinated me, bad luck at cards, and then it was a woman in Paris—and now, the marihuana. The weed! The extravagant, the lovely weed! And what it has been to be a weakling going with every wind that blows. . . . But I had the weed, and that has been like the trumpets and the choirs of Doomsday to accompany me. Ah, but it was worth the while, señores—what has been my degradation, my loss of caste but a poor sacrifice to cover the ecstasy and the bitterness that are mine, what were the paltry years of misery to pay for the happiness I have known—it was worth the while, gentlemen. I have found life whole, I have found it complete, everywhere—perhaps, I have found even the Fountain of Gold.

"What dreams I have had, and what times! Yes, I have been king for a day with a whiff of the weed, and I have lived in a pigsty of a *jacal* with an Indian woman, but give me the weed, and I am whole again, I am a poet, I am a man! I am a greater poet, look you, señores, than Calderón de la Barca, and I have the marihuana. Well you may laugh at this beggar in rags before you, mumbling and incoherent, but look you, señores—you, gentlemen! and I had not found the contentment and fury of the weed, compared to which all other sensation is as dust, I might have been that poet great as Calderón de la Barca; yes, in Mexico and through Latin America and even in Spain, who knows . . . but what I might have been the last great voice of gold?

"The weed is like the lotus, and it is the weed that counts, and not the poetry. You smoke it, and all other pleasure and beauty compared to that the marihuana brings become stale in the mouth and heavy on the heart. And you smoke the marihuana, and you take a long siesta with life, a long pleasant siesta, free from care. It is the dream and the smoking that count, and not the living. Ambition fades to nothingness. I have been frantic with fear and lust and rage under the influence, when I willed it, and I have known peace that none of you shall ever know on earth, and I have been lost, utterly—and seen in evil such beauty as only the profane can see. And yes, I have killed a man in exotic hatred, and laughed to see his blood drip through my fingers while I tore out his living heart like a high priest of Montezuma on the crest of Teotihuacán. And I shouted as his body rolled down the temple steps to the nest of vipers at its base.

"I have painted like Michelangelo, like El Greco, señores—I have known that ecstasy, that peace and beauty which is Art. I have sung like Caruso, hah! I have been rich and complete when I had nothing but a pair of tattered breeches to my name and no shelter on the beach at Vera Cruz. Why should I write, paint, who had but to live? And how could anything in life be as beautiful as the marihuana? Where, in sober life, would you find such make-believe, and what is life but a dream within a dream? I had the marihuana.

"I have sailed with the great sea captains of all time. I have been a bullfighter, like Gaona. I rode in the night-raids with Pancho Villa, that last man to strike for melodrama in our dull world. I have been in the front of his cavalry, like Taillefer, the first to strike a blow and the first to fall, chanting the Song of Roland. And I have been an exquisite, deadly, I have torn the leaves from red roses, and watched while beautiful Castilian maidens were raped by brutal Negroes. I have been in a Mohammedan's heaven, surrounded by houri.

"I was with Cortés—*I remember the white towers and that island of Tenochtitlán*—I was Ortiz the Musician when Cortés entered this kingdom of Mexico, four hundred men we were against an empire! Or perhaps I was called Sandoval, El Buen Jinete. I was with Maximiliano at Querétaro, that gentle Emperor, and being Mexican I was the first to betray him, the first to despise his unfortunate Empress, and the first to be sorry because we shot poor Maximiliano in the face. I have been at many great and dramatic moments, witness to things that would keep you listening for hours, if I had the time—ah, if I had the time, señores! What dreams, what it is to smoke the weed, señores. . . ."

13

"In one sacred area of that city," he continued, "there were a great many people, a multitude . . . but they were like statuary—they were stalled, in the motion of walking in the square, or they sat talking with each other on the onyx benches, their mouths half-open in astonishment, or they bargained in the markets, and yet it was a waxworks of a city!

"And as I walked past I imagined they talked of me, they whispered as I passed, and though they were spellbound and their slanders were only in my mind, I was afraid. I tell you, señores, such a multitude will cause you terror like the unseen, the incredible, the phenomena beyond the grave. I wanted to escape their uncanniness, the presence of this living dead, this terrible game of charades —so I entered the principal temple, I remember it was shaped like a pyramid, like something in the Old Testament or the golden city of Babylon—but I had not passed the portals for its doubtful sanctuary than I drew back in fresh horror from what I saw in that vast vaulted chamber. There were a thousand people—like *penitentes,* on their knees, pitifully, señores, hushed and bowed in that temple before a high priest who sat on a throne. They seemed to live and breathe and worship hopelessly.

"A thousand people petrified, hushed forever in a moment of worship, dead, motionless, frozen—what is the word that I can say of them? It doesn't sound terrifying, but I can tell you, as I looked on that sea of bowed heads, their humble mien was a terrible whisper, an accusation I wanted no part of, the most living thing I felt in that horrible city—they looked the most abject savages in this world, and their humility lingered like anathema—their mysterious penance vibrated in that chamber. It arose from their mass and silence like a gentle breathing—and I would not have touched one of these people, brushed against any if I'd had the sanction of the Mother of God. Perhaps it was an old piety that protected me in my peril, but then it might have been—that the enchantment died a thousand years ago.

"There was a seraglio that you entered by draperies of spun gold, and this was weirder still—it was filled with indirect lighting from underneath a burnished dome, the flowers were waxen like orchids in a jungle, *they looked poisonous*—and tropical birds were everywhere, but they did not sing. It was a great harem of temple maidens, and scores of lovely women lounged there, all of them remarkable in that they were blondes with golden hair that fell below their waists, and fine blue eyes like clear water, and the brave laughter that would not be heard again in the Western World. They were like Valkyries, the music of

Wagner. Perhaps they had been sent as tribute to the monarchs of the Western World from the Greenland colonies a thousand years ago—for they were Vikings, and they were beautiful, the tropic sun had never touched their loveliness. There was peace about their eyes, and they were the golden thighs of Paradise. The sight of them affected me with a bitter nostalgia, and again I remembered, as we all remember, what the Spanish have lost in the Western World.

"They were like the blue-eyed, golden-haired Spanish descended from the Visigoths, that we all in our subconscious remember. It is not that we are people dark by nature, attracted by the light, the tall and the fair; it has been with us since we first came to the Indies, that we suffered a fall from grace—for the Captains of Cortés were massive men with red beards and light hair and blue eyes and voices like Thor—and we would remember the Visigoths. We have a bitter nostalgia for blondness, we brown little men, we yearn back to our ethnos, we would dream of the fair people with blue eyes, that even the Indians believed in—and we have remembered the Visigoths.

"They were very beautiful, these maidens of the temple. For they were maidens—and how they had languished, far from their north country, for their Norse people, for love, for pity since. They were asleep a thousand years, and on their cheeks were tears. Their lips were parted in angels' breath, and I was struck with pity, with a pity that rang aloud in my heart. They seemed to breathe, softly, they were too beautiful to be dead. They had cried themselves to sleep a thousand years ago, and now there was peace in their eyes. Christ, it was terrible, señores, it hurt—this thing touched my heart, it rang on my heart like a hammer on an anvil. *O madre dolorosa,* how beautiful they were! What had they done to deserve this exile and death? It was fantastic, it was good as something out of *Amadis de Gaul,* it was in the new world a thousand years ago, but it was a Gothic tale, just the same.

"When I think of those women with the tears on their cheeks, old as I am, I grow faint with the thunder in my veins, I am blind with desire, I hear the dim disturbing music of haunting cathedrals and my spirit is pale. Something in my heart expands and contracts in a vastness like the limitless notes of a bugle down the wind, or I die of desolation like a fallen leaf in the autumn. They were so white and pale, there are men among you who had cut their throats and not known the reason why—they were so *white,* señores, *so white.* Like the throats of *gauchipin* women—that is what love is, gentlemen—the lip-bitten fierce lust—look you, it is more than catching a wench behind the corrals at night and throwing her down violently, grunting and wrestling, but these things, doubtlessly, you will not understand. Because you do not remember the Visigoths, you do not have the murderous lust after white throats, nor is there the music of lost cathedrals ringing in your ears.

"Yes, I have looked upon such unearthly creatures, and I came away, and I came away feeling that I should do something about it, that it was expected of me to lift this enchantment, with a sign of the Cross, or a touch to their brow, but the very idea gave me a cold sweat, and I came away from the temple maidens and I found myself in the streets again, rushing through the streets of that awful city, the people crying havoc, for they seemed to cry after me to stop and heal them with a Christian benediction—

this was what they had been waiting for, a thousand years! They seemed to cry after me, piteously, but I thought I was mad. A thousand years, the dead, the unburied, and they cried after me! But I ran. I imagined the dismay on their faces, I dared not look at them from fear and shame, but they cried aloud, at last. There was a babble of voices for a moment, and then silence. They had waited for a Christian a thousand years, and I ran.

"That is how I acted when I came face to face with the Improbable, with the Improbable that is the commonplace of the gods, as though I didn't see it for shame or terror, and what excuses I have made afterwards, how I have tried to salve my Christian conscience! They cried after me, gentlemen, and I heard them—but I ran. I wanted only to save my skin. I hurried on at a trot, like an Indian, when I could not run from exhaustion; panting and panic-stricken like a beggar being drummed out of town, through the gates of that forbidden city, over the causeway like an urchin enveloped in his grandfather's coat, past the fishing boats stuck in the lake like flies in molasses, and I came to the foothills and scrambled up them, still in a panic. I ascended the great mountain that was a wall of this moon-struck capital of the Western World, scrambling and crawling.

"The underbrush and jagged rock tore at my clothes, when I looked down the steep incline my stomach turned over. My hands and feet bled from the climb, my muscles ached intolerably! I panted with dread and I chuckled with the devil's delight at my escape—I fancied all I had to do was clap my hands, and the evil city would disappear —I shook my fist at it, and I laughed. I laughed and laughed. What did I care if thousands perished, if thousands were never delivered to grace, I was safe, I was safe, *do you understand?*—I was back on the mountain, away from that evil dream of a city. I laughed like an idiot, but that is all I remember. I was struck from behind by an unseen hand and I fell like an ox, and then there was darkness, a blank unpeopled darkness.

"When I came to, I was in a goatherd's camp in a pleasant valley, the mountains towering above us like the Andes. I had been sick for weeks, delirious, the good man said— my muscles ached intolerably, my eyes watered still—in fact, I'd come stumbling from the direction of Torreón raving with fever, laughing like a *pobrecito,* and the goatherd had to strike me, O Excellency—he said, he was a very old man, and he used the expressions of colonial days, Your Worship and Excellency, and Madonna for ladies— that he might bring me here to treat the fever that was destroying me. With wild herbs, nothing more, O Excellency; never fear—I would get well, completely.

"I thanked him, and offered a few wretched pesos I had about my person, but he was a very backward man, he had never been out of these mountains, and what need had he of silver, O Excellency? He lived with his goats and dogs, and his only diversion was in the evening to play on a rude-fashioned reed. And sometimes men came to barter with him from Torreón.

"I made discreet remarks about what lay the Other Side of the great mountain, but he said nothing, nothing at all until I came to the valley of Maltrata, where was farmland and a pueblo. He could see these places from the mountains, Malpais, Maltrata, every name about the land seemed to be *mal, malo.* He was rather a simple old man, he thought Maximiliano was still the Emperor of Mexico. He

had spent his life in the *montañas,* he knew them all, and I did not argue with this grand primitive, shaggy and good as a dog, Homeric of head—I was not well, I assure you, but I had the sense not to discuss an enchanted city with a simple goatherd—such a person, used to living alone in the mountains, can frighten so easily, and destroy one!

"Ah, señores, you have believed me, I can see it shining in your eyes. *Señores del campo,* the gentlemen of the plains, I salute you! You look like the men of Cortés when they heard of the gold in Tenochtitlán, and the men of Pissaro who went into Peru. And I did see that strange city, believe me, you cannot take the memory away—else, why should my belly crawl with terror at what might have been a bad dream, or why does my heart lust after the white flesh I saw only in a delirium? It is all very easy to say, this did not happen, that is not true—but it is to deceive yourself, and who are you to judge? It did happen, and in the fashion I have described—I stumbled on that city lost in the dimensions of Time, forgotten in the memory of man, and I can remember the white towers, and the red beserker sentinels, and the pale skin of the temple maidens. The gods have been good to me, señores, but I have amused the gods."

We fell silent as the ragged urchin of a man finished his story. We had heard a lot of stories, but never one like that. ... He snuffled and he shook with the ague from his marihuana, or it might be he had malaria. Depend on it, the little man had not touched our pity, for healthy men despise the weak and the deformed, the poets and the minstrels like this one, but it was curious—it was strange, and we knew better, that none of us wanted to consider him a liar.

He pulled at his underlip, it was a Hapsburg of a lip, and he hadn't cared, anyway. For he broke down, as these people who smoke the weed very often do, impossibly balanced creatures, and he cried; he cried like a baby, it was that shameful, but even Javier had sat quietly and not said a mocking word.

14

*Ay, ay, de ay,
canta y no llores . . .*

IT WAS THE FIRST SONG I heard when I stepped across the river into Nuevo Laredo today, it lingered there like an old love refrain. It was on the juke boxes, always followed by those perennial Mexican favorites I seem to remember years ago, 'Deep Purple' and 'Stormy Weather' and their own *'Guadalajara,'* and I went into the Alma Latina and sat in the patio where I listened to the sad *mariachis,* four Mexicans dressed despondently in *charro* costume, and they sang the *'Cielito Lindo,'* accompanying the song on their guitars, *ay, ay, de ay, sing, don't cry,* their falsetto voices lingering, they sang the *'Cielito Lindo'*—the Pretty Little Sky.

I never grow tired of it, either. I pay these *mariachis* to play different versions, it has been such a long while since

I have heard it—I sit under the arbor in the Alma Latina and I listen and drink tequila sours and I think of old times. The ghosts are here in the Alma Latina, I could listen to it over and over again because it reminds me of so many things, this beautiful folksong of Coahuila, and listening to it I am carried away from this stinking border town, all the bitterness and the disillusion and the ugliness seem to fade from this land I want desperately to love, that I have loved in my heart, but that I can't help but despise in the abstract. (And a mist of tears would come to my eyes as I remember—*ay, ay, de ay, because singing, you will gladden, Pretty Little Sky*, such who are sore at heart as I. And I look back on the days of my youth dimmed with time, and I could weep for those days, and this bitter land.)

I loved it then, even this ugly border town, when I was young. It wasn't as ugly twenty years ago. Or it might have been the same, and the difference was in me, because I had the high heart then, and I was young. And now the illusion is gone, and all the people are sour. I listen to the '*Cielito Lindo*' in the dirty patio of the Alma Latina and it is sweet as ever, plaintive as the sigh of a breeze through the juajillo and huisache trees, and I can't help but think nostalgically again, that was a long time ago, and this is another country.

It wasn't always like it is now, Nuevo Laredo used to be a friendly place. Then you didn't have to put up with the heavy-handed *turismo,* the shills and *pachuchos* and people on the street you wouldn't like to touch with forceps, the eternally disappointed gringos, the footsore American females on the make. It was a different country in those days, Mexicans and Americans even liked each other. We had good times together. In fact, my best friend was half

Mexican, by the name of Hugo Corrales, one of the dissipated young men, the rich lost young men of distinguished family who was staked out as a sort of remittance man on the frontiers of Tamaulipas.

Hugo never knew whether he was coming or going, but he didn't care, he had a good time. He used to talk whimsically, and say it was a sad thing, and that to me he could talk like a brother, but it was a sad thing to have the heart of a Mexican, and the head like a gringo. It disturbed him, it was always getting him into scrapes, he seemed to be betrayed constantly by one of his turbulent nationalities or the other, and once he had been exiled from Mexico for leading an abortive revolution. But this period Hugo enjoyed characteristically, having had his father pull wires in Mexico City to appoint him the Mexican consul in Hollywood. Mexico didn't have a consulate in Hollywood, but they made one for Hugo. He came back with a platinum blond bride, naturally.

Hugo was a good man to know in Nuevo Laredo in those days, he was a person of consequence. Even the shoeshine boys did not pester Hugo, and the lottery vendors kept their leprous distance. He and I used to tear up Nuevo Laredo about once a month, when I came in from the ranch with a terrible thirst. You got to Nuevo Laredo in those days, and you wanted to raise hell. There was something in the air. You felt the raw good freedom of Tamaulipas by merely walking across the river, you were an expatriate by simply crossing a bridge, an honorary citizen of Mexico, and you didn't have to buy your liquor under the table. Mexico was a charming and rather primitive place, then; utterly unsophisticated, ripe with sentiment and humanity, never bored—there was a pattern to follow, black was black, and white was white, you knew what to expect; it was all that simple.

I can't remember a time when I was more vitally alive, or had more gusto, but we were young, then. All Hugo's friends were mine, without question, and he had many, and what times we had together! What vast meals of *cabrito* and *guacamole* we consumed in those days—you had indigestion after every meal, or it wasn't considered good —and what a host of friends I really had, who have had so few friends since! The amazing thing was that men could be comrades then, it was before they were apron-strung or the pansies spoiled all that—in those days a man was your friend really, or he didn't want any part of you politely, it was that simple, and Hugo and I met our friends with *abrazos,* with never a thought of being stabbed in the back. Nowadays, you don't see the *abrazo* very often in Mexico, and when you do, it is a half-hearted, empty gesture. But we had friends in our time. (And how many tequilas and Carta Blancas we drank at the Alma Latina and the Cadillac and Shamrock, and how we hated to leave good company in those days, and what fine words we had spoken —lost words, never to be recalled or written at all, but the best words nevertheless—and how it had been good to be drunk in Nuevo Laredo when we were young!)

We knew all the answers then. We used the high brave words. We traveled in strange exotic lands from cane-bottomed chairs under this arbor in the Alma Latina, and none of our real travels was ever so good as one of these. What wizards we were, we must have been wizards to have made life enchanting in this stinking border town. *Ay, Nuevo Laredo! Ay, Méjico.* . . . We heard music that only the drunks may hear from the strings and lips of beggar-minstrels, and we found a strange stark beauty in low company and what is regarded as Evil. We lived among cutthroats and whores and found their company honorable. They were just like everybody else, only a little more human.

Ay, and the fights we had—with gringos and Mexicans and all comers—it seems we were always fighting, as young men we were willing to fight at the drop of a hat. And the police always let us off with a wink or a bribe to their chief, while they indignantly put the other parties in jail for disturbing the peace. *Who said the Mexicans didn't have a sense of humor?* And the women we laid, fine brutal women, the love we demanded arrogantly in those days, the Youth breaking out all over us—even the books I put by to write another day, because in Mexico it was the living that counted and not the books, and who wanted to write books when he could live?

Yes, I can remember Nuevo Laredo kindly, twenty years ago. Now I don't know what is wrong. It is the same ugly border town, but I look around and all my friends are gone—or they are rich and successful, the ones that are alive, but I don't think they are happy. The ones that write can't write as well as I can, if that is any consolation —they get paid better, and they don't get drunk any more, but they can't write. And I think as I hear about them, that I wouldn't trade my misspent life for all the Success in the world. I would do it again if I had back that Yesterday, and I shake hands with myself because I wasted that particular Yesterday—nobody can take *that* away from me—and I can remember Nuevo Laredo as it was, and as it should be, and kindly.

It was one of the few times I was really alive, there were

no sour grapes and there was no looking back. And I remember there was a vague peace, too. And how the moon shone in the patios of the little cantinas after most of the patrons had gone, and the skies had been clustered with stars, and somehow that little item is significant. Ah, the peace of those moments, rarely, the well-being of the present and the promise of what was to come that night or tomorrow or another day, that nostalgic peace I remember and that I have never known since, that we have never known since, Hugo nor I! And yet, it all happened in this stinking border town. It all ended in the bottom of a glass, with our mouths dry as alum.

Hugo and I used to start drinking in the morning before the cantinas were cleaned, we pushed open the swinging doors and smiled at the bartenders—their places swarmed with flies and smelled like urinals in the morning, but we had fires to put out that literally consumed us, and we would drink beer cocktails, full of crushed ice, until a little of that Peace came back again. Life was all right, then, even with a hangover—it was nothing that a bartender couldn't fix in a few minutes, because we were young and healthy and Youth is a love of intoxication in one form or another, and we took the easiest way. By midnight, we might still be across the river, doctoring that hangover, drinking the *penúltimo* tequila—we never used the word *último* in our lives—and it was fine, God was in heaven, and all was well with Mexico, with Mexico.

And why do I remember these things, sitting here with the *mariachis* playing in the Alma Latina twenty years later, when I have had triumphs of other sorts, pleasures, times when I was real in other places, honors even, and more respectable pastimes and subtler intoxications—but why do I remember this Nuevo Laredo as the best, what rare distilled ecstasy was it besides Youth that Hugo and I enjoyed in those days? We didn't give a damn whether it rained or shined, we weren't ashamed of our vices, and we were glad to be drunk always, and whatever has happened to the border since, we didn't miss our cues in our times, Hugo and I had the best of it, and perhaps it is just as well that those days are gone forever. We can remember them, and we have them forever. It didn't matter, so long as we had the tequila and our dreams that never came true and good talk and our illusions and our friends, Hugo and I were complete, alive in this wretched border town, we were real. We could have our cake and eat it too, in those grand days—it was better than any Bohemia! We weren't ashamed of either intoxication or sentiment. And now there is too much justice, and all the people are sour.

15

W<small>E COULD DRINK ALL DAY</small> for five pesos, and Hugo had credit everywhere, in the saloons and stores and *congales*. He was a remarkable young man, the more high-handed and arrogantly he acted, the better the Mexicans liked him. He was their last young hidalgo, and Nuevo Laredo was proud of him. He was just as welcome in the underworld as he was in the high society of Monterrey. I never got in trouble as long as I knew Hugo. He got me out of one amusing but slightly sinister scrape that I have never forgotten. I had been drinking at an obscure cantina on the outskirts of Nuevo Laredo, by myself like a fool, just soaking up the local color I thought, and since it was in the redlight district, the bartender fed me a Mickey.

Later, a whore picked me up in the gutter, where I'd been rolled. I had been robbed of my money and clothes and left shivering in my shorts. They left my passport carefully beside me, though—that was the whimsical touch, because Mexican cutthroats can be considerate, even courteous, if it doesn't cost anything. I woke up shivering and helpless, and blessing the bastards because they hadn't left me entirely naked, gurgling and choking from the drug, and my first thought was that I wished Hugo was here, so that we could go back to that dump and clean it out. I laughed at the idea, I was still laughing foolishly when this girl picks me up out of the gutter and tows me to her mamma's. I was muttering and slobbering; I was that confused, I didn't even know the girl was a prostitute. I remember protesting it was improper to meet her family in my condition!

I was so dazed I didn't notice how lovely the girl was until next day, and then she looked good, she looked like a cinema actress, Lupe Velez even. Not overstuffed like the Mexicans like them, but slender and firm. She had cold black eyes, black hair, and that tawny skin and warm laughter. She was always laughing, chattering like a parakeet, and I didn't pay any attention, she didn't expect you to—I listened to the lilt and refrain in that warm lovely laughter, and I made love to her because she was always ready; I mended under her care, in a couple of days I was good as new. I didn't find out until I was ready to leave that I was a prisoner in that whorehouse.

It was too priceless, because things like that didn't happen to real people. I was actually to be held for ransom, like any tourist, and I thought at the time that of all the absurd things that ever happened, anywhere, this took the cake. But I would go anywhere for a laugh in those days, it was one reason that people said I didn't have character.

It didn't occur to me to tell these thugs I had influential

friends even among the police, I let it go with hollering for the United States Marines and a few battleships. All they wanted, they very patiently explained, telling me to shut up, was five hundred dollars, American money. I thought it was a gag. They might have been the same people who gave me the Mickey, I don't know until this day—but if they were, it was a sweet racket. I was in their clutches another day before Hugo discovered my plight through some underworld grapevine, and when he practically kicked down the door, he was great—he had those unsavory characters, the one-eyed madame and the assorted pimps in the kitchen, crawling with the tongue-lashing he gave them.

It was really beautiful to watch Hugo lose his temper, he could dress down a *mozo* or a slovenly waiter to perfection, and I always marveled afterwards that the waiter didn't spit in our soup. I have never seen anything like the abject apologetic attitudes of these small banditti in that house of ill-fame, they trembled as if from blows, they implored Hugo for mercy, until I felt rather sorry for them. They hadn't known I was a friend of Hugo's, Oh pardon them! *Miserable sinners that they were,* but Hugo didn't let up on them until he had turned the knife in the wound several times, although they knew all along that he would not turn them in to the police. They were frightened, out of respect.

I can't say they mistreated me the several days I was held captive in that absurd whorehouse. I was given to understand, but very politely and whenever I was willing to listen seriously, that if I didn't come through with five hundred dollars, American, they would find a place to bury me in a shallow grave along the Monterrey highway, and nobody but the coyotes would be wiser. My body would be washed out by the rains in the spring from its shallow grave, but that was no way for a Christian to die. Wasn't my life worth five hundred dollars? I couldn't believe all this threat and menace was real, they were so pleasant about it—and it was like something baroque that might have happened in the last century, along the Camino Real in a more Gothic time, but not now, in Nuevo Laredo, where I was even a citizen of consequence. And it was fair, they reasoned with me—didn't I have money to burn, being a gringo and rich, and they were poor people. They even offered to reduce the ransom. And besides, they reasoned not without a point there, hadn't they thrown in the girl for nothing, *pelón?* I was really hard to please.

It was that priceless, they carried on their blackmail and menace and kidnap with perfect courtesy and good humor, and all I had to do was ask for a drink and get the best they had in the house. The one-eyed madame cooked me up some swell *menudo,* which is good for the hangover. She seemed to have been the mastermind behind this childish racket, but she wasn't particularly evil, she was easygoing and rather motherly like some of the best female slayers of our times, and the several *mozos* that hung around the kitchen didn't look tough, there was something wheedling about their entire attitude. They liked to talk about everyday affairs, they seemed good-hearted souls. And yet, even if I tried to poke fun at their racket, I was not such a fool as to underestimate them. I could hardly believe it was quite real, although I knew that more than one body of a gringo had been washed up from a shallow grave on the Monterrey highway.

I could write a book about the whole bunch, and that

lost weekend I was held for ransom in a whorehouse in Nuevo Laredo, but because there was little drama to the characters, nobody would believe me. They were just plain ordinary Mexicans, the pimps and waiters could have belonged to a union, from the way they acted. I can't write a close-up about that place, Hugo and I didn't hold anything against these people, I even wanted Hugo to let up as he tongue-lashed them, I felt particularly sorry for the one-eyed madame who was shuddering like a tubful of jelly. We took the cinema actress with us, when we left. I can't really describe that experience, except that it seemed a little unreal. All during this shabby adventure, I remember, I had expected for some reason that a tourist guide would pop in with a crowd of schoolteachers.

The last time I saw Hugo he looked like a death's-head. He was dying slowly of a cancer of the throat, nothing but skin and bones to him, and what griped him most was that he hadn't been able to drink anything stronger than coffee for years. And this was the same Hugo who used to think he could drink all the liquor in the world, and lay all the women! It was pathetic, in a way . . . but what the hell, he said, the rest of them were dead, all dead. They were all dead, anyhow, or they might as well be. We two were the only ones alive, we were the last, but we were alive and kicking, and who wanted to live forever? And at least, we were dying principally of our sins, and not our virtues.

While the rest of our generation, and peace to them— none of them lived to be over forty—were dead, all dead. They were all dead—of alcoholism, of the climate, of the long futile rage called *coraje,* of frustration, from making too much money or not enough, worry, getting married too often, overeating, blown prostates, insanity, God knows what else, they were all dead, anyhow. They died like lambs, but at least, we were dying of our sins, and not our virtues. Some of them died pillars of the church, Rotarians, of their very worthiness even, and they all died before we did—and without the tequila and the good times, or the travels we had in the cane-bottomed chairs, or the fights and adventures up these dim Bohemian alleys, or the women in the *congales*. Even the wives of those men didn't love 'em. And because at heart Hugo was gentle, he felt sorry for those poor bastards.

And it is true, we are alive and kicking, after our fashion. We still have an eye for adventure, we are not ashamed of sentiment. We have lived too much, but that was the time to live, when we were young. We haven't regretted a moment of it, we'd do it again—and we had the best of it. And yet it is a little sad to think of Hugo dying. There was a time when I remember he was *muy hombre,* he could raise more hell than any two men on the border, fighting or drinking or loving. I remember, too, the afternoon he jumped into a bull ring, exasperated at the cowardly *novilleros,* and fought the bull with a white handkerchief, much to the delight of the crowd, for everybody knew Hugo, from the cutpurses sitting in the sun with the whores and throwing beer bottles at the matadors, to the *buena gente* and the fine ladies sitting in the boxes, he was the sort of scoundrel everybody loved.

He refused to Work, God bless him—he used to kid me because I did, but Hugo was too busy living to Work. And his brothers, serious men all of them, supported Hugo rather enviously, if the truth were known. He even brought lustre to the family name, and it paid, because every time there was a revolution in Tamaulipas, the property of the Corrales was never molested because Hugo was so popular with the common people. (And I looked at Hugo dying piecemeal, and I remembered how he used to blow everything on wine, women and song—and how he used to go to bed with three women at a time, because Hugo was gregarious, and I think it wasn't a bad life, it was exciting even if it was short, and at least he is dying at the tail end of his time on the proper page of the proper chapter of the proper book, and I'm not—there was never anything inconsistent about Hugo, and at least he is dying in character, of his sins, and not his virtues.)

I sit here in the Alma Latina, listening to the sad *mariachis* sing the 'Cielito Lindo,' and I get a glow from remembering Hugo and those times. From remembering my friends in the dim cantinas, the drinking tequila together when we were young, before our illusions were gone and all the people on the Mexican border had turned sour, and I remember the journeys we took on these cane-bottomed chairs here in the Alma Latina, the dreams we had and the fine words we had spoken—lost words, forgotten words, never to be remembered or written at all, but the best words nevertheless—and the friends we had everywhere in that golden age, gone now, every one of them except Hugo and I haven't the guts to look him up—ah, it might have been an ugly country, even then, but we had the high hearts and we saw it through the bottom of a glass.

16

THE BULL RING in Nuevo Laredo is stuffy and resounding, it expands and contracts with excitement, it is glaring and shoddy. But once on Washington's Birthday two of the greatest bullfighters in history fought here. They fought the same day, Gallo and Silvano. In the spring, in Nuevo Laredo, with the brave bulls, the bulls of caste from Spain. Silvano who was always spectacular, and Gallo solid as Babe Ruth. It was a great show, this tourney between those two matadors, *mano a mano,* it was a brave day, in fact. The hysterical crowd would not let you forget it, there was a din in the *plaza de toros* that made your spine creep.

People were yelling as soon as the parade began. The picadors led off to a bugling like war, on grotesque horses, gaunt and emaciated beasts that were lame and blindfolded and padded, but ridden cock-horse by these medieval lancers in leather aprons and iron boots and brown derbies. In the center of this spectacle, like some contrast of magnificence against poverty, were the matadors with their flank of capemen, all brilliant in that staring day, the contrast in front and behind them, because bringing up the rear in dead earnest, democratically, were the real knight-errants, the red-coated porters with fresh haircuts and frogged tunics and their clipped bay mules that were used to drag off the carcass of the bull in the end to be butchered and distributed among the poor.

Bullfighting is a spectacle, not a sport. It is full of that contrast, a little raw perhaps, but beautiful and stylized as some Catholic ceremony—and once you get over your gringo prejudices, it seems nothing but a rather rude and healthy holiday, bread and circus to these people. The drama is a man pitted against a dangerous animal, and who are we to call it brutal, who pay good money to see two prize fighters beat each other's brains out? The *aficionados* have a lot of biting things to say of that sort of Fair Play.

That afternoon was full of suspense, as only a *corrida de toros* can be, because it is the last drama of our times that has death as an immediate object. The crowd was wild, these people were there to acclaim Gallo, without reservation and like good nationals, the greatest bullfighter in the world. On the other hand, they were not loathe to seeing him killed. There was a thunder in the music and the laughter and the shouting, awe in the tumult of their voices, and all of it was for Gallo. They didn't care for Silvano because he was born in Spain, but they idolized this rather stout individual who moved about the arena with the same light-footed heaviness of the Babe playing baseball. They were prepared to idolize him so long as he was the maestro. And in my judgment they were right as rain, because Gallo was a great *diestro,* he was the greatest living bullfighter—the splendor fell around him in the din and glare and he deserved it, even if he was just a middle-aged, beefy man in scarlet and gold and purple, always smiling, enigmatical, a little mestizo.

He killed the first three bulls without effort, and they were good bulls, raised by the Duke of Tovar. He did it elegantly, he did it well, and when it came Silvano's turn, the crowd would not have Silvano, they wanted Gallo to kill all six bulls, and they would have ignored the second greatest swordsman in the world, they wanted Silvano to go away. They threw cushions and other missiles into the ring at the Spanish matador, with no malicious intent at first and good-naturedly enough, but when Silvano would not take the hint they grew indignant and soon were out of hand and acting like spoiled children. They clamored for their favorite, and when he would not reappear, indifferent to this demonstration and wanting to be fair to Silvano, the crowd got into such a pet it began to throw beer bottles and look around in the wooden stands for something to tear apart. The bottles began to fall around Silvano like hail, and furious at this treatment, sullen, with his matador's gorgeous honor at stake, he refused to retire, he called for his bull in a voice that could be heard above the tumult and the shouting.

He was a matador always mad, fighting mad. The bull came out at him with a rush, and Silvano faced the unharried animal, that had not been caped, or goaded by the picadors, and to the amazement of the crowd but at the same time against its very grain, this insolent Spaniard taunted the great beast with exultant cries of *Ha! Toro!*

Ha! Toro! while the people screamed invective and continued to throw beer bottles. He was fairly skipping to keep them from bouncing on his shins, while any cushion, if it had hit the matador, was enough to break his neck. A man had to be brave in more ways than one to be a matador in those days.

There Silvano was, side-stepping the bottles and dodging cushions with a spitting contempt—you could see him spitting out the side of his mouth viciously—in danger of his life from the fury of the crowd, but nevertheless he received the charge of this fresh bull and with one clean thrust of his sword he dropped the brute in its tracks. He twisted his body a little to one side at the last, but until then he received the bull coming head-on like the old *diestros* received a bull, and he drove the sword home, and the bull fell down on its knees bleeding to death, and Silvano turned grandly and dismissed the crowd with a gesture, and the beer bottles stopped falling.

It was a fine thing to see, a rare thing, a brave thing to see—this matador turning his back on the hostile crowd and killing a pure caste bull fresh out of the gate, and a few people did jump to their feet, hollering that this was a man, to give him a chance, but this only excited the crowd and those people were yelled down, and one man who continued to yell for Silvano with what the Mexicans admiringly call a head like a burro was even assaulted, and the police took him away for creating a disturbance. *Ay, Méjico,* it could happen only in Mexico! The Mexicans are that charming and inconsistent. The crowd was willing to begrudge it was a beautiful and brave thing Silvano had done, he had turned the tables on these people to the perfection of Spanish scorn, but they would not have any

part of him, they wanted Gallo all afternoon, and when Silvano withdrew, with one contemptuous salute, the third finger of his right hand stuck out wickedly at the crowd, it roared with rage, it became infuriated all over again, and the beer bottles smashed against the exit gate like ice tinkling in a glass.

The people cursed and sulked, they seethed and hissed over the insult that had been put on them. They began to moan for Gallo, they put up a veritable Wailing Wall for Gallo. Their faces were uplifted in agony and loss. They would have started a riot, but their idol appeared before they got out of hand. Gallo appeared reluctantly, as if all this were getting monotonous. The people subsided then, like the sinners they were. The music blared, the next bull was turned out, the horses were gutted in a trice, running around the arena kicking pitifully at their entrails, the great matador's retainers scurried over the barriers, some of them with difficulty bearing off a fallen picador who could not rise in his iron hostler's boots, and everybody agreed this was a bull light and efficient, worthy of Gallo.

When the ring was cleared the bull gored the dead horses, pawing the bloody sand and bellowing massively, but when it looked up and defiantly around, there in the center of the ring was Gallo, alone. He had been there all the while. The people were so delighted with the bull they had forgotten Gallo, but he stood there regarding this pandemonium with perfect indifference, like a small tradesman in the plaza, smiling, enigmatical. He had a cape in his right hand on one fat hip, he was never a colorful man, but he moved out against this blood-crazy bull with a rare grace, with all the dignity of a brave man, a good man who was never afraid to die.

The bull saw him and leaped to the fray, and for three minutes there was a melee of twisting bull and matador, the crowd gasping as Gallo used his own special *verónicas* on the beast time and again and to perfection, apparently doing with the bull what he pleased, and taking the utmost risks. He did not look like he was ever in danger, except once when he slipped on a patch of blood-wet sand. He fell rather awkwardly, but he lured the bull by with the deceit of the cape, and he was up on his feet again with a surprising nimbleness. After that he gave the bull every chance, but the bull had met Señor Gallo. Gallo was so graceful and expert with the bull that it looked like the beast did not have a will of its own, but was a trick bull, especially trained for Gallo. But all that was Gallo's confidence, his negligence and daring.

It was said he had never been brushed by a bull in his life, never tossed, that Juan Belmonte was the only other *diestro* who ever fought in as close, but the *aficionados* shrug at the comparison, because Juan Belmonte was a cripple, he *had* to be brave. Juan Belmonte was a very fine gentleman, and a Spaniard, but he *had* to be brave. Only Gallo gave the bull a whiff through his daring.

Gallo extended himself that afternoon, it seemed he would not be outdone by the brilliance of Silvano, he made the fast furious beast follow every pattern known to matadors—he then experimented, he improvised, he made new expressions and designs with the cape and the bull and himself in the arena. He was a great artist with the bulls. And watching Gallo you realized that bullfighting is an art, it is the art of Spain, and it is enough, because in it are the cruelty and the glory and the chivalry and the blessed fatalism and the high disdain. It is a surface mirror and a tradition, and it can be fascinating as a duel, grim and satisfying as vengeance, graphic as contrast, beautiful as a ballet of death. At the same time it can be the Conquest and the lost Armada, the secret of Spain. It can be a spectacle of life and death, and as Gallo interpreted it, it can be the bravest and the fairest thing a man can do to live and die. And it can be an empty gesture, and when it was, Gallo was so negligent, he risked his life in such a manner that you wanted to cry out against the extravagance.

The great matadors are always histrionic. They have something in their heart like pageantry. Watching Gallo you forgot he was just a fat little man in scarlet and gold and purple, who owned real estate in Mexico City and loved his family and would not fight on either side of a revolution, for you were on your feet with the crowd, as if an unseen hand had rubbed the hackles of your spine, and you were screaming *Viva! Viva!* at this fat little man. There was a great heart in that beefy little body. And you had the odd sensation that the rest of the people had, that you were sharing this bull with Gallo, that you were even fighting this splendid bull yourself, and doing it as well as Gallo, and that in itself was enough for any man to accomplish in a lifetime. For just one moment, the world was big enough for any man to get away with what he was doing well.

Gallo passed the bull with *faroles* and *chicuelinas* and *gaoneras* until it backed off winded, flickering its tail like a great cat, at last wary of its sinister opponent, and then Gallo, like a small boy—almost with his tongue in his cheek

—played a little comedy, at drollery with it. The bull was intrigued, he didn't know what to make of it all. Gallo was like a pleased child teasing a gigantic saurian, and the crowd roared with delight. This was a mood of Gallo's they had never seen, and he was pitiless about making a fool of this brave bull, this brave honest bull, until it looked like he intended to make a travesty of the matador's profession. At the last he got down on his knees before the bull and melodramatically threw wide his arms like a foolish and vainglorious *novillero,* humbling the great beast that had cleared an arena, until the bull seemed bemused and disgraced. It just stood there flicking its tail, urinating, looking at Gallo curiously, as if it were hypnotized. It had probably never seen a clown in its life.

Gallo tantalized it with *molinetes,* and with the point of his sword he exhibited its charms in broad pantomime after the sly indecent manner of a flesh-merchant, and suddenly it even occurred to me that this greatest matador in the world would also have made a great *padrote.* Ha! and when he was tired of that role, he pretended he was riding cock-horse, and you saw the bull as a horse, such a horse as is ridden in Chapultepec Park, in Mexico City, with Gallo pointing derisively at the bull's rump, a mile across the beam, like the Mexicans like the rump on a horse or a woman. It was a crying shame to treat a good bull like that. . . .

Gallo had this dishonored brute stalking him cautiously, like a great cat about to pounce on a roll of yarn! Then to everybody's amazement, he turned his back on the bull, he walked over to the barrier and sat down on the rail and took out a silk handkerchief from somewhere and wiped his brow delicately. When the bewildered bull came up to him, lowering, Gallo put his cap on one of the bull's horns. It shook the cap off indignantly, but it didn't gore Gallo. Then the matador got up and stretched, yawned, and finally walked away like a man who has finished a cigarette. He refused to kill that brave bull, and even the bull was disappointed.

    He had built the crowd up to some sort of finale, and then Gallo had walked out. The bull just stood there perplexed, flicking its tail and urinating, looking after Gallo, and when the exit gate was opened for it, the bull trotted out of the arena like it wanted to go home. And the crowd would have cheered, but they were perplexed, too. They didn't know what to think in the crowd, but all those people in the grandstands had a sudden inglorious feeling that Gallo was pulling their leg, that he also had dared to despise them, that he had discovered their secret shame and cowardice, and that this greatest swordsman in the world had made a travesty of all he held sacred, not to ridicule the bull, but themselves. Not to ridicule the bull, the bull was his colleague. And the cheers stuck in the throats of that crowd, a great hush fell on these people. Gallo got under their skin, and for a moment they wavered between revulsion and indignation—you could feel their indignation crawling in the stands—at a loss how to save face. It had been a letdown for them to have acclaimed Gallo as they did, to have shared this experience with Gallo, they could have fawned on him for the favor—but he also let them know what he really thought of them, in the end. And he let the thought fester, and the thought was, that Gallo liked the bull, he admired the bull, there wasn't anything wrong with the bull.

    And to cover their embarrassment these people threw

their hats and coats and valuables in the ring, like children when school is let out. There were a few broken cheers, but for the most part the people were silent. It was something the Mexicans had not seen before, and it was something you never heard them mention afterwards, and they got up and quietly walked out of the grandstands, because they were at last ashamed of the way they had treated Gallo's great and good friend, Silvano.

17

NUEVO LAREDO IS A DUMP, the rear end of the universe. It is ugly and deteriorated and degenerate, and on the surface of it has a dullness, a drabness almost hideous, yet underneath this veneer, underneath its vice and its glaring boredom the extravagance lies, the extravagance is there. Always there is a suppressed excitement about Neuvo Laredo like a shout about to burst from its lips. The *grito* is always there, just about to be uttered. The extravagance—the day before yesterday, for instance, that fellow Judy. It was all extravagance—extravagance and waste and a pity, but that is what happens to all the stories I find. Life isn't a bed of stories for me. The richness spilled out of this one, vague, elusive, tantalizing, the background was there, the drama was there, it began with a bang, but it ended, like all stories based on life must end, with a *phftt*.

You meet these queer fish in Nuevo Laredo, they are

always drunk. There is something in the air, all right—you hit this desolated border town, and the first thing you want to do is get stinking, the first thing any man wants to do is to get drunk. This guy was just as smart as anybody, he said he was a correspondent for the *Picayune,* and we were sitting on the cane-bottomed chairs in the arbor of the Alma Latina, drinking tequila. He was working his way back to New Orleans, drinking his way up from a revolution in the banana republics.

He was a young man with a crew haircut and malaria. He had the jitters bad, but he was used to the fever after five or six months of it, he said. He had this strange tale to tell, and he practically held to my arm like the Ancient Mariner. His name was Mike Judy, and he had been down in Honduras. Nuevo Laredo was civilized compared to it. There had been three of them to go into that jungle, he and Hogan and Talterwaithe. Hogan was a tropical tramp, black Irish, but Talterwaithe didn't have any business in the tropics, he was about twenty—he was sweet, Judy said. From what Judy said, he was down in the tropics for a lark.

That had been a lark, all right. Talterwaithe and Hogan were still down there, they weren't coming back, either. They had joined up in Tela, and they were sent overland with a carbine apiece and dispatches for Feliz, who was the professional soldier in charge of the revolution for the deposed president Gómez. Feliz was an Austrian, with a price on his head by every government in Central America. Feliz was a happy name, but his real name was Von Salm, and his grandfather had been aide-de-camp to Maximilian in Mexico. The newspapers said he was a sadist, that he killed and robbed, and raped women in the sacked towns because nothing in life was violent enough to stimulate him any longer, but that was what the reporters saw through their beer. Feliz had a bad press, that's all. Judy said he was really a mild stoop-shouldered, middle-aged officer with a short predatory beak like a parrot's and green eyes with no expression in them. And he didn't spend his spare time lying in the mud and stench of that forgotten land thinking of the cool frail beauty of some woman he'd loved in Vienna, either.

Judy tossed off another tequila with a lick of salt and lemon, and looked at me blearily. It didn't cost but a nickel to buy him a drink. I ordered up, because he was singing.

He and Talterwaithe and Hogan had walked two hundred miles through Honduras in search of Feliz. The *Message to Garcia* was mild compared to it. It was a beautiful land, though, part of the way. They picked breakfast from the banana and papaya trees, and they drank the milk of green coconuts. The natives were sullen and unfriendly, Negro and Indian and Spanish all scrambled together—so the three men had to forage, and after the first robbery they looked behind themselves guiltily and timidly ahead at the great forests and greater silence.

Then the fever struck. It was quick, and it hit you like a pestilence. And after a while they seemed always to be wandering in the crazy mountains, standing on the eternal brink of a new wilderness, or fearfully entering the little towns that swelter in the jungle. It was bloody, Judy said. Christ! it was bloody. That was a word he had picked up from Talterwaithe. The fever shook them, it jangled them, and they went skulking along, afraid of their shadows. They moved slowly in the tangled undergrowth, it tore at their clothes like bramble. It took them a day to go three miles, cutting their narrow path with machetes, but that was when they first started, that was record time. A day seemed forever, they felt they had been in that jungle for years, and in that jungle they would stay. The trails closed behind them as they crept along, there was a finality about it.

They wrapped their feet in sloth-hide when their boots were worn, and killing those pitiful animals had been a little like murder. The sloths clung to trees squealing until you cut them down. Hogan's face was swollen like a comic balloon. Mosquitoes ate them alive, their bodies were covered with ticks, chiggers burned in their feet. It was damp as a well. They sweated like men in a Turkish bath, and the farther they went the weaker they became. The roots of the trees sprawling on top of the ground were larger and more grotesque than any they had seen—it was a nightmarish land, stinking with evil. They walked with their mouths open, like idiots, but it was to breathe.

They passed one jungle and then mountains and went into another jungle—and they were lost. Deformed trees choked and bent by vines, with the damned bindweed everywhere like fishnet. It was the fallen bindweed that made the stagnant pools of straw. And they would step on slimy things that made them shudder. They almost starved to death. There was never a sound in the jungle. There never is, Judy said. The sickening moths made their leprous supplications as the men passed, and it was like going into some slapstick silent initiation into hell. The ground was covered with dead insects. The flowers contracted themselves in sexual palpitations. Their sweat was rank as musk—they were very beautiful, and absolutely poisonous. The nights in that jungle were silent, too. There was nothing in that jungle but solitude and mist and dawns that barely illuminated. It was like a cathedral, Judy said—not a bird, not an animal stirred in the gray cathedral light. You knew that monkeys and parrots and great cats and boas were there, but you never saw them—they were silent, like the jungle. They were hidden by the impenetrable foliage. It was like a buried temple, where God looked in through a peephole, but you couldn't see the skies. Animals and savages lay there listening, and their silence followed the three men like candles snuffing out down an aisle-way.

The slosh of their feet as they trudged through the rotten straw was like marching, the hack of the machetes in the bindweed made a weird lonely sound. Fright and the stillness descended about them like an enchantment, until they became meaningless, and they stumbled on in a nightmare. With the fever heightening the illusion of their madness, making the terrible desolation rich and choking. It was awful, Judy said, to be alone like that, there were three of you, but each one of you went shaking mad with the loneliness.

Then they were out of this jungle, and over the mountains, a hundred miles, a thousand miles it seemed—in the rain. It rained all day and all night. To walk in a trail was to walk in water up to your waist, stagnant, deadly to drink, the foliage rotted in it, like sewage. The hardships you suffered were incredible. If they had not been out of their minds they would never have survived. For they must have been mad, quite mad, towards the last —they moved along like sick men, in a dream. They nursed their carbines like dead little babies, and sang little songs to themselves. They were always singing little songs to themselves. They were frightened of everything, of animals in the night and animals that were not there, of the mountains falling down or the huge forests crashing flat, of all the natives they saw in that land, of a thousand dread and imaginary spectres, besides. The madness followed them out of the jungle like a ghost, and they recovered slowly from their fever in the drenched mountains.

And Talterwaithe, who had come for fun . . . he talked incessantly, in that high cheerio voice, like something out of a bad English novel. Always about his eternal trip down from New Orleans. It had a fascination for him. "I came to the tropics," he would repeat, "on a boat smuggling contraband. It was actually a schooner, with sails, and that was more than I expected—we sailed west at first, and then we were on the Caribbean for a fortnight, in a fog. We sailed along the coastlines, the porpoises racing and sounding at the helm, and we anchored in mangrove swamps at night, avoiding the dirty little ports, naturally. Sometimes the fire-tree, and the insects that illuminate it, cast a glare like a bonfire on the schooner as we moved out to sea. Those foul little ports were unreal, anyway. Too childish to be real, with a castle-front on the wharves and the houses in pink, mud-gray, saffron, all the colors of the sickeningly sweet drinks the Indians take in the market like paregoric. There is something rather pathetic about those Indians drinking *dulces*."

And whenever Talterwaithe repeated this part of his insistent narrative—it was like a phonograph record, over and over again—Judy would think of the sweet tamales, rank coffee, cheese and sour butter and frijoles and mole

that were offered for sale in the plaza, and his stomach would turn. There was nothing on his stomach, but the green bile would come up anyway. And Talterwaithe would go on idiotically, pedantically, almost as if he wanted you to repeat what he said: "We sailed down the coast where the jungle grew to the water's edge like gigantic stagnant weed, the boat leaking and the food enough to give a man scurvy, but it must have been a beautiful sight, to the natives—to see that white schooner, for instance, lying on a green seaweed sea in the mouth of a jungle river in the twentieth century. There was something grand about it, it was good as Conrad."

Like hell, Judy muttered, in the Alma Latina, but Talterwaithe was sweet. Judy grabbed me by the arm again, and he said, you never saw such a ham. Judy hawked and spat on the ground like a Mexican and hollered for a drink, and he said, *like hell,* again. He was droll, that Talterwaithe—and yet that ridiculous recital seemed to keep him from coming apart at the seams, he repeated it over and over like a litany. And Judy and Hogan could have killed him. Judy said he used to listen, staring at Talterwaithe out of hollow eyes, wondering if Talterwaithe were crazy. That's the way it is, when you are crazy yourself. And Judy didn't know if he were crazy right now.

His eyes were clouded, and he was really drunk, with the fever and the tequila there seemed to be a few disembodied versions of himself walking to and fro in the patio. He didn't want to talk, but he had to—he is probably still trying to tell his incoherent story somewhere, somehow. For all I know he might have been crazy, the malaria and the drunkenness were certainly peeking out all over this odd jangling young man, there must have been an intolerable ache in his bones and a ringing in his ears enough to drive him crazy. At times talking to me he would look startled, as if he had heard a bell or perhaps a dog-whistle, and then he had a look in his eyes like the four walls of the cantina were crumbling in the patio, and he said that the crazy mountains were going to fall, that the mountains were falling down, just as they used to sway and teeter and crash on him and Hogan and Talterwaithe when they took that damned *Message to Garcia*. They were supposed to get five dollars a day. Well, there wasn't any Elbert Hubbard to write about *them*, Judy fairly shouted, and some of the patrons of the Alma Latina were staring—not that they cared, or were ever surprised at gringos drinking tequila, for gringoes can't handle tequila.

It had been like discovering a lot of thieves in hiding, Judy said, when they came to Feliz' camp. What a happy name that was, it had a lilt to it, Judy said. There was no sentinel posted, because no enemy would follow them into such a jungle. And those bushwhackers were sprawled in the stale jungle dying like flies of typhoid and fever and *chorro*—or it might have been, of the damned bananas. Even the horses ate bananas. And the queer thing was, the whole of this army looked upon him and Talterwaithe and Hogan as still stranger and more miserable creatures than themselves—after all, to be laughed at by scarecrows, it did give them a turn! Even Gómez came out of a banana-leaf hovel to laugh at them. Everybody laughed like hell, and there didn't look like there would be a laugh left in that whole army.

Hogan and Judy and Talterwaithe were nonplussed, they stood there trembling with shame, crusted with filth

—it helped keep off the insects—skin and bones of men, ragged and bearded and sick, looking for any kind of welcome. But Gómez made them a speech, instead. He was a kinky-haired, potbellied little black man. He wheezed for air, his huge belly corseted with cartridge belts. To hear him laugh was a terrible thing, somehow. It was a loud gut-splitting laughter, Judy said, and it made you want to hide.

Gómez made them this little speech, with his damned tongue in his cheek, he fairly pulled their leg. He came romping out of that banana-leaf GHQ with his hand held up in salute, like a potbellied Mussolini, and he put on this act in public. It was better to be a lion for a day, than die like a dog, he said. It was dog-eat-dog in the jungle, though, and not good to be wounded, either. If you did not die of the gangrene, the only mercy you could expect was the *tiro de gracia*. And just because they were gringos and had a touch of fever was no reason to act like tramps off a tropic boat in Tela, with their tails between their legs.

Buck up, he said, they would learn how to be men, in Honduras. He was just a potbellied doodlebug, Judy said, in epaulettes like a rear admiral, his dirty stomach showing through a dirty shirt and a blouse that would not button, his barefoot staff of Negroes grinning behind him, but do you know, Judy kept saying, you know, the peroration was fine! He was a poet, by God—the black bastard, and Judy said this seriously, he painted the ochre walls of the village, the orchids in the patio, the silver in the cupboard, the women in their nightgowns, until the eyes of the Negroes would shine.

That was a queer sort of war down there, in Honduras.

The enemy tried to fight by the rules, they dressed in uniform, they looked like a Balkan opera—they shuddered in their boots deliciously, hunting out the ragamuffins of Gómez and Feliz with bugles and glory. They came marching into the jungle in order, exasperated at the rebel cowardice, taunting these scarecrows, but they never came out again. It was at night, or when they were marching back through the awful silence, or lost, that Feliz fell on them and dispassionately destroyed their detachments to a man. Or Gómez had them all hung kicking in the trees. That was the worst part, it was pretty bad.

Judy couldn't get over those poor bastards kicking in the trees. The comic expression on their faces, as if this could never happen to them! Judy didn't want any more of that bushwhacking, not in the banana republics, anyway. The way these bushwhackers hollered *Arriba! Arriba!* as they pulled at the ropes, and even the officers clung to their captors for mercy. Even the officers were almost affectionate with fear. And again Judy put his hand on my arm like the Ancient Mariner.

Then he became incoherent, just like that. It was as if the tequila had crept up behind and slugged him. I caught a few words, about the officers being affectionate with fear again, the wounded crying in the night until the Negroes went out, white-eyed, to finish them. And something about a weird and brave and useless cavalry that splattered down in the mud before the machine guns, or tried to herd its infantry up and riding down the men who faltered like police whipping little boys—but then it was all a bad dream, anyway, a bad dream about children. I sat in the patio of the Alma Latina, drinking tequila with this shaken intolerable young man, and he began to mumble, mumble, mumble, like a phonograph needle caught in a rut of a warped record.

I asked myself if it made sense, and why I was always picking up with characters like Judy in the dimlit patios of these Mexican cantinas, and why a perfectly good story always had to end like this, why a story that began with a bang had to end with a *phftt*. Here was this miserable young man getting so drunk on my hands that I was embarrassed for him. The twilight was falling, and in the distance I heard the bells of a cathedral. The rest of the patrons of the Alma Latina had gone home for dinner, there were only this intolerable young man and myself in the patio, drinking tequila. He looked like he was going to break down any moment, and since there didn't seem to be anything I could do, and because I could not understand a word he was saying finally, I got up and I quietly came away. And I went to my boardinghouse and up to bed and I lay there watching the shadows swim around on the high ceiling, and it took me quite a while before I realized the man was a liar.

18

It was twenty years ago, in Monterrey, that I met the dark Barbara. She made everything I had imagined or read about Mexico true—it was all there, the extravagance, as I have attempted to show, the cloth of gold, even the *femme fatale,* too vivid to put in a book. The women in Monterrey were very beautiful, but they were common garden varieties, they were tasteless, they were as nothing, I tell you, as the stars when the moon shall rise, once you met the dark Barbara.

Her youth and beauty were legend, twenty years ago, and yet she was not young. She was timeless and mysterious. There was a song of bitter triumph in her siren's eyes, or so the poets said—her lines were those of a Greek statue, she was Samothrace and she was Helen, and the first time I saw her I said, *O Soul, is she not fair!*

She was tall and very dark, with black amazing eyes that were shattered in prisms like black diamonds. She had gipsy hair, and the faint mustaches that are considered marks of beauty among the Spanish. She had the nose of an Assyrian queen, and she walked like a harlot. She was strange and wistful, with absolutely no humility. She belonged in a time when all the women were proud.

Her father was a Dutchman from Surinam, and her mother a descendant of the viceroys of Peru. She had a name that would stretch across this page. There was a great coat of arms over the grilled doorway that led into the beautiful patio of her home and, Spanish fashion, this was located in the tumult of the main square where you could hear the bells of the cathedral boom. One moment I was in the rude bustle of the street, pushing through the crowd in the colonnades, but when her door was opened I walked into another world. I passed through the ancient grilled door, under the golden coat of arms, and I was in the quiet and stillness of a hushed patio where the only noise was the singing of exotic birds, and my senses were enraptured by the aromatic flowers. There was nothing but marble in the patio and the halls. For a moment I thought I was in a colonial town a hundred years ago, in a time before the heart of the world was dead.

Though her family was wealthy and owned half of Nuevo León, and her mother had a great Spanish name, the girl had no suitors. Only Hugo and I ever went to see her, and she treated us like brothers. She was disdainful about her ostracism, she did not care, she was too proud. She was mysterious and unattainable, like some princess in an enchanted wood. Or so the poets said, they were romantic in the Alfred de Musset tradition, and they wrote in French, or if they used their native tongue, they wrote like Rubén Darío, and they said of the dark Barbara that she was haunting as lovely music, maddening like the intolerable Andes, and part of the dim tropics like the weird flowers are. To them she was absolutely gorgeous, and perfectly deadly. She was all women to all men, a myth and a dream they would follow and never find. And the facts were, and this was said reliably, that because of the dark-haired lovely Barbara two of the very finest young men in Monterrey had blown out their brains.

So it was true, you see, everything in those days was true. Here was the *femme fatale,* your flame for a moth, here was a woman to take your breath—you have my word for it, I cannot describe her to you, she was too heartbreakingly beautiful for a book. There was a hush when she entered a room, she was like the stillness before earthquake, and she *was* like the intolerable Andes and the lush devouring tropics. The stars were like a cloud when she moved in that extravagant patio, and you heard strange music when you looked into her eyes that were shattered like prisms. To possess her had been the end of a man's desire, and yet I was attracted to her as if she were a beautiful novice kneeling at an altar, the cross of gold on her breasts, singing, singing! Her beauty was nameless, all that the poets said was true—everything that was written by the poets is true. It was a long time ago, in another country, but it is true.

I loved her in spite of the shame attached to her like a loathsome tabu. There was a very realistic side to her legend—it seems when she was seventeen and her family lived in Surinam, she had an unhappy affair with an escapee from Devil's Island. It is always a Frenchman in

Latin melodrama, and it is always Devil's Island in fiction. He was not an ordinary man, he had been a famous artist in Fontainebleau before he cut a woman's throat from ear to ear because she was ugly and he was tired of her, and probably crazy as Van Gogh.

He had long curly blond hair that came to his shoulders like a Visigoth's, and the gentle expression that always brings out the best or the matter-of-fact in a woman. He made a meagre living in Paramaribo by selling figurines carved from the soft cedar, but they were lovely things and very cheap. He hung about the streets, a ragged and romantic figure, sleeping in doorways, and certain of them were opened to him in the night, it was said, by the very best ladies in Paramaribo. And lo, our dark Barbara, this Laura and Beatrice and Deidre whom Hugo and I worshiped with tears in our eyes, she had taken pity on him, and pity being what it is in a woman . . . there you are.

She had been so kind to this rag-tail unfortunate, it was rumored about the cafés in Monterrey, that the artist was soon peddling images of a nude figure, and it was the Grecian form of the seventeen-year-old immaculate Barbara the artist used for a model, the most beautiful woman in the tropics. The face had her unmistakable patrician nose, the form had the brave, breath-taking Grecian lines. He must have been crazy, or he was hurting, or it might have been as the gossips said, a Frenchman would prostitute his own grandmother. His motive was unknown, but soon afterwards, naturally—these matters can be arranged on the equator as they can be arranged in Monterrey or for that matter in Randado—the ungrateful convict met a very rugged sort of assassination, and the Dutchman and his family moved to Mexico, far away.

You can't escape disgrace in Latin America, however, and theirs followed them about like some primitive curse. A loss of face among the Spanish people will follow a family from country to country, and one false step by a young girl can accurse a family for generations. If she had been a sister to any man in Monterrey, or even Hugo, he would have killed her, to wipe out the stain on the family name. But the Dutchman loved his daughter, she was the most beautiful thing in the world, and perhaps because she was half Dutch and thus foreign, the people in Monterrey had forgiven her—and it was only at the Casino and among the Americans that the continual scandal grew—and in their Quixotic way they were even a little proud of the dark Barbara they sheltered with their pride. In some lands she would have been shunned for moral turpitude, condemned by her sisters whose morality is largely expedience, for the worst of being a pariah is to be patronized by pariahs, but she was accepted decently enough in Monterrey. She was proof that the Spanish can be generous, that the Spanish can be lavish so long as nothing touches their pride.

The Spanish people in Monterrey were even gallant about the dark Barbara. You could never slur her to a man, there were even duels fought over her honor. The men seemed to warm their hearts by her beauty that fairly shone in that dim colonial town, they acted as if she were the last candlelight of Christendom. She was their madonna and their talisman, and they were her champions. No smug leer or hideous lechery pursued this soiled and beautiful woman, no man in Monterrey was sly or disrespectful in her presence. There, indeed, was your forgotten age of chivalry! They would tell you about her, but you had to hold your tongue.

And if your heart went out to this lonely woman, and you wanted to take her away, if you were willing to live in disgrace and exile because of her fatal beauty, as I was then, that mood would pass, for it wasn't the custom in Mexico. The Spanish make their beds, and they lie on them. And you knew, even if it were regretfully, and she knew, being half-Spanish herself, that she might go with you to the ends of the earth, she might even love you a while in return, but in the end she would despise you for the sacrifice you made, and because you had violated her bitter pride.

Perhaps she is dead now, and I think of her too, here in a cane-bottomed chair of the Alma Latina, drinking tequila with my memories, or maybe she is fat and jolly like women get in Mexico, her almost fatal beauty faded into flesh and garrulity, the legend forgotten until tomorrow or another day—this legend of the last *femme fatale* in the Americas, in this dull world in fact—but she was magnificent once, in her day, I tell you she was magnificent, and I don't even like to remember why I know. And if you don't believe me, you can go to Monterrey, for the fact remains, that two of the very finest young men in that town had put bullets in the roofs of their mouths and because of her.

And I think of her legendary beauty, and I can never go back to Monterrey.

19

Last night I said goodbye to Margarita and Ernesto and the good Mexicans at the cantina off the walled ruins of San Juan. I heard the last story I shall ever hear from the lips of the Old Men, and probably it is just as well, because nobody cares—it was a long time ago, and nobody cares.

"When Little Juan was grown to a lad," Ernesto said and he continued his stories like they were often told, "it was strange, each time that the brush became twisted and gray, when the wild geese came flying and honking over the fringed *laguna,* he would be up and gone to a far country. He could no sooner think of staying had the padrone been dying, or poor Isabel, his fiancée.

"And only his mother seemed to understand, it was the wild hare in her own blood. She was not surprised the first time Juanito left us, and did not return for eleven months. He must have gone like the Indians go, to have eluded Diego and Domingo and Valentine. They had tracked the ladino all the days of their lives, but they found no trace of Marina's son. They came back on a bitter dawn, the dew dripping from their ponchos, the sweat steaming on skinny horses—half-starved, exhausted, but Marina cursed them until they were sick and trembling as from blows. She was a witch when she wanted to be.

"Little Juan was a strange lad, a moody one, with odd quirks in his laughter that made you wonder if he were not tormented by some madness. *He laughed as a man laughs at something later.* He was an utter fool about horses. He was not happy unless he was with them, they had more allure to him than tales of fair women. He was *muy caballero*. He rode entirely standing in his stirrups, señor; like a man about to make a cast with the lariat, which is well and good, but the buttocks were made for the saddle as surely as the horn for a lasso. When he did sit, *faintly*—he had a gringo balance and could feel the smallest thing wrong with his horse's mouth or stride; when, Jesús, half the time we can't feel a horse going down until he is piled on top of us.

"He ran wild horses for the fun of it. He rode in rain and sandstorms and over frightful prairies caught in fire. His real love was for riding like the wind in the brush by himself. He didn't mind hard work or useless danger; yet if you should ask me, we like smooth going and poky herds of cattle and gentle horses and cowcamps to sleep in as a steady diet, though we never get them. But Little Juan would go out on moonlit nights and sleep needlessly under the stars, crazy as a woman, when everyone knows that the moon will cause loco, and fever, and when he knew that any man of us would swap places with him at home and sleep in a nice warm bed for once if he so much as mentioned it. He would go yelling and urging after wild cattle in the high *monte* as if he were the devil behind them, and as if that were more fun than sitting in the patio drinking and feasting. If I had been Little Juan, believe me, I would have done nothing but sleep and fill my gaunt belly out and quench my thirst the rest of my days. But Little Juan would be with us holding herd when the blue norther was blowing so hard we had to kick and quirt the sullen men into their work. And all the while, he might have been in a warm room, stuffing and drinking. That is what I couldn't understand.

"This lad would grip a horse between his skinny knees, and ride him to death. What would you think of that?" Ernesto asked. "He was peculiar in a lot of ways. But when he grinned in his apologetic, half-forlorn fashion, we did not begrudge him the pitiful thrill he had from the horses. He was sorry—afterwards. His horses were spoiled and petted, gentle as lambs under his hand but nervous and excited whenever he left them with a groom. This pleased Little Juan; he wanted one-man animals—wild, vicious, ornery horses that would have a fit if anyone else even looked at them. He used to have the *peones* beat and torture his mounts until they were five years old, and then he would step in with his frozen smile and dominate them, with spur and quirt if necessary, but mostly with kindness. And that is a deceit that even a horse will believe, Mother of God! He got his one-man horses, all right. You see, he was the first and last man on earth who was ever kind to them.

"If you say he was a coward, you're wrong. He wasn't

afraid of anything, and you seldom meet a horseman who isn't afraid of *some* horse. When you are afraid, you can't fool the horse. You can walk up to mount when his hind leg is lifted and the men are earing him down and he has a blindfold over his eyes, you can use your best poker face and be confident and easy and have an air about you, bully and slap him about—your hands may not shake and there may be no fear in your eyes, but somehow down deep within you, if you're afraid, the blindfolded horse is going to know, even if the men don't. Something quakes in your soul, and the horse feels it. He knows your moods like nothing human.

"There were six hundred horses on Don Juan's hacienda. You'd go into a brush lake to flush the cattle, and a stampede of horses would come out instead. They would chase the cows and kill the goats, and when they couldn't think of anything else to do they would go thundering around in herds of thirty or more, laughing and kicking up their heels. The imported stallions would charge us any time we got within sight of their brood herds, jealous and vicious and wild as a flame. If we could jump off our mounts right quick they would stop short and go snorting back to their herds. If we kept running, scared out of our wits, and if they ever caught us as we went whacking brush and jumping pear like we had never done before as long as we had lived, they popped horse and rider over as if we'd been caught in a *mangana* and went whinnying back to the mares with their tails in the air and their slim necks arched.

"And Little Juan had great hunting horses as high as a man sitting a Spanish pony, that could jump a five-foot corral and breeze over barbed wire fence as if it were chaparral. He would take these horses out with a pack of mongrel hounds and hunt down coyotes and mountain lion. He would start early in the dawn and sometimes not get back for a day or two, with those fair brutes limping and foundered and half his hounds killed by wild boar. And every time a horse was hurt in the brush it would mean a thousand pesos out of the old man's pocket, but Don Juan never said anything but *Juanito, Juanito* . . . as he shook his head."

Ernesto frowned; and he studied his empty glass until I had it refilled. He had drunk a quart of tequila by that time, but his hand was steady, his mind was clear, and he could have eaten an entire *cabrito* if he'd had the price of that delicacy. The room was filled with smoke, and it stank of body-odor; the candles guttered out, and there was left only a lantern hanging over a table where some beggar sprawled in the corner. The young men were gone.

"But Little Juan," Ernesto said, "was not complete, he was not whole, *pobrecito*. We were all very tender towards Little Juan. He had been a wild lad, *ay*, but by the time he was twenty something had gone out of him. He would not even bother to fight like other men. It was very sad, señor. He would stand by and watch while Tomás Sabinal did it for him.

"Tomás was his *bruto*. No one knew how old Tomás was, he was bowed and stooped and nasty as a tarantula. I remember a whole herd of cattle stampeding wild-eyed by him in the night, climbing over each other and knocking down men on horseback, but they split about Tomás like water will around a sandbar, and he stood there slapping them past with his rawhide chaps and whooping like a fiend. Javier said they didn't run over him, because he smelled so bad. Tomás was one of the old-timers; when he got his big foot caught in a stirrup he would not get panicky, but grab hold a mesquite and between him and the horse pulling they would break the girth or a leg, with no hard feelings. But forgive me for straying, you must pardon if I talk of men I can better understand than I did Little Juan.

"He made no sense to us, señor—riding, like the wind, like the haunted. Only his touchless pride gathered the frayed ends of him. He lived in another world, and strange confusions came on him out of *nowhere,* and then, some white laughter. *He laughed like a man laughs at something later.* He was not whole, poor lad; though he explained himself until his voice might ring in the dark cantinas—we listened, and we loved him tenderly, like a son, but for all we heard, we might have been listening to the wind blowing softly in the mesquite and juajillo outside the door.

"There was a tower in San Juan," Ernesto said, "I don't know how high it was, it is crumbled now. It was higher than the cathedral in San Luis Potosí, people said, and from the top of it the old Don was wont to light his beacons in the early days to call his men from the plains. It was a great square structure, some forty feet by forty-five like a granary or a fortalice, but furnished inside like the abode of a Spanish queen. Time was when they used it as a grand hall for the *baile,* or merely as the place for storing munitions and machinery, but inside it was dim-lighted, the heavy draperies on the gray stone walls seldom drawn to allow the foolish sun to enter from the sentry-box windows. It was dim-lighted all of the time that Isabel lived there.

"A wide stone stair wound steeply up from one flight of rooms to another so that the sight of the high length of them was never lost. The rooms were bare and dismal and aloof, but somehow that tower was rich and well possessed. It was cool in there, and quiet at all times as the whispering huisaches at noon. There was always a gentle whispering about the tower.

"Moving in this quiet, with an Indian lass or two but no Christian to visit her in all the world, and yet pampered and spoiled in this lavish severe house was the loveliest lady who ever lived between the Nueces and the Rio Grande. Her hair was black as a mustang's hoof and long so that you might feel it would fall over a balcony rail. She had lips that never smiled, and her eyes were black and serene as those of a nun. She dressed as the padres do, in long brown robes with not a rope girdle but the woven silver belt the Seminoles make, and on this were the keys to many rooms she moved among like a chatelaine.

"And we, who like our women of the earth a part, to go with their masters in fiesta and poverty, to be a plaything like those in cantinas are, and a cook and housewife, the poor man's servant, and the mother of children as well —what is there we loved about Isabel? She was frail and beautiful and useless, and more like the Virgin than a woman. She was always *still,* señor. Only her hair moved in the wind when she stood on her balconies. And she might stand for hours facing the mountains, or disappear like a shadow does. There was no noise in the tower but the clumsy clumping of her Indian maids, but this was welcome, for it broke the utter enchantment.

"Isabel and her brother were orphans, they were the only survivors of the Kiowan massacre of the people at the hacienda of Pablo Reyes. They'd fled in terror with a great wolf-hound to protect them. Valentine found them cowering in our brush, two days after the massacre. They were brought to our village when Isabel was four and Enrique five years old, and Marina, that good woman, raised them like her own children. The girl grew into a beauty, but the boy had a stricken look that made him appear weak and cowardly.

"Isabel was the betrothed of Little Juan from the beginning, since the time in boyhood he became aware of her loveliness. She had a strange sacred beauty, even as a girl. He wooed her properly with presents and tenderness and words golden as those the minstrels sing; they kept the whole village awake with their serenades, when the time had come for courtship. It was he who called her *Isabel,* by the gringa name.

"What if they were lovers, long before the day their wedding was to be? They were but creatures of God, after all. We did not talk, we did not dare, they were our *queridos*—don't you see? There was no rendezvous in the corral at midnight, or the grunting and passion of *peones* that amuse us in our cups so much; we had nothing at all to say of this affair. And they thought that no one knew, but faith, we, every soul, in the village knew. We could see his slim black shadow scale by the hanging vines of the watchtower to the high overhanging balconies of Isabel. The world could see, every man of us, if ever we lifted our sullen glance from the earth and looked at the tower shining whitely there in the moonlight. But we were afraid, we did not like it, and we sat in the close indoors or spat on the ground and lowered over our cigarettes and the things of the day.

"For Enrique found them out, as we had expected. He was delicate and quiet like his sister, and crippled in his mind, *pobrecito,* but he was proud and quick about his honor as any other man with Spanish blood. The night that he and Little Juan fought on the high balcony, all the village was hushed in fear, with every eye straining up at them. The moon was bright as the day for us to see, while they fought like tigers with knives for claws, wounding one another horribly, until they fell to earth locked in each other's arms—and Enrique was stabbing our padrone's son until they hit the ground. He had hidalgo's blood, that Enrique—and that affair had taken all the fight out of Little Juan forever. It was a miracle Little Juan lived, but Enrique died at once. Isabel had uttered a single scream as she looked down on them that night, and fell in a faint that was nearer Death.

"For ten years then, she lived alone, but for her Indian maids. She accepted the costly gifts that Little Juan brought her from the ends of the earth, but regally—like a priestess taking earthly things. She was still lovely as the winds that blow the blossoms, but Little Juan did not climb the stone tower again. She moved like a fairy queen in a treasure house, all day.——Waiting, perhaps, for that high white tower to fall.

"But once in a while, of a glaring moonlit night, she came on her balcony out of that bare and lavish house, and she sang the songs of Spain. And the whole village would be quiet like animals hushed to hear the mockingbirds in a moat-lake, and she would sing for hours as if her heart would break, or she would stop after a song like a bird in a cage.

"She was a captive there, señor—*the insane live such a long, long while.* She was mad, you know, as mad as the village idiot was who went galloping, galloping after the dim *corridas* on his broomstick horse."

20

THE OLD JESÚS MARÍA was an idyll, a colonial dream violent and colorful, with bitter things to love. There had been dry days and fern-like juajillo and huisache shade with the yellow blossoms fragrant as the scent of a bride. There had been immoderate thirst, until water was like wine and the taste of it cool and desired—and hunger, until one wolfed the fresh-killed venison and beef, indigestible, half-cooked, and belched like a vaquero and called it good. And drank the damnable coffee that Esteban used to make, that gave a man heartburn all day. The living in the open, sleeping on a saddle, riding unbroken horses in the brush and roping wild Chihuahua cattle, with the lariat tied fast to the saddle-horn—it was a fine time! Out in the sleet and rain and dust, it was a good cruelty, a young cruelty and joyous —the cattle stampeding through the night, the horses dropping dead underneath us, hardy horses, able to go twenty miles at a gallop and all day without water, captured from *manadas* that ran wild in the Great Barino country, breezing through the valleys and the tall grass like a prairie fire. Those horses were grand, they fascinated me—and because of them, O my country, I could almost forgive you the thirst of torture!

And the vaqueros were fine, a rough cheerful lot, primitive and cruel, killing their horses in the *mogotes* after the wild ladinos, risking their necks every hour, but anyone would have thought from their raw laughter, it was a lark. They had been great *compañeros,* violent and faithful and unforgiving, thank God! Now they seem odd and incredible as I look back on these splendid men, weird like everybody else in this country—riding into black dawns that illuminate like a revelation or across mud-splattered plains with the thunder come upon them like a frightful enveloping or masked in the dust behind herds of cattle, figures in a dream almost, singing, always singing.

How they rode, yelling, *O-wee-baa, o-hee, o-hee!* in their high voices, and hell-for-leather over the gopher-eaten prairies, somersaulting through the air like steeplechasers when their horses stepped in holes or were caught in the *monte.* They waited in the deep shadows of the brush, *I know, I know*—for the sabre-horned cattle, the thump, thump of a pony's heart beating against their boots, and these cattle they tangled and tied in their lariats, and were in the saddle again, crashing through the deep brush, hallooing after their companions like men hunting stag. It was enough to make the rest of my life an anticlimax. It had been a raw time, a fine day, the good days—when we were young, and lived dangerously.

It could not have been more feudalistic in the Middle

Ages, and yet it happened in America, in the twentieth century, in the lost world. It was where I got the Chateaubriand complex, but it was Youth, it was Adventure just the same, and I found it at my own front door. And years later I have remembered those times—and now I write of the Jesús María at last, of the long drives to the railway, of a vaquero's spree in the stinking town of Pena, where we drank prodigiously and fought over gringa whores, and as the young padrone I had my choice. It had been heady stuff for a young man, and I had been impressed with myself, I had not been human were I not confused and delighted—everything was mine for the asking, enemies done to death if I had them, every door open and the ladies to be had for the ravishing—and oh, it is true, it is simply true and nothing more, that I, exquisite young man, I had found it for the most part, tedious!

Perhaps I had wanted something else in my poet's heart, I don't remember. Peace, perhaps; I dreamed of peace as the good padres do. I had been bored until it was dear, it had been sweet at the end of those long days to return to the Jesús María, the ever-lovely and crumbling Jesús María on the great *laguna* where the huisache spread its green and yellow scattered lace . . . ah, no one who has never ridden for weeks in the yellow glaring day where all things are limned pitilessly as by the first early processes of photography; no man who has not hungered and thirsted immoderately, and dreamed foolishly of Youth and Love and Beauty, can ever understand the suffering affection and the sense of loss and need that I had for that twilight village of the Jesús María in a violent land!

Perhaps a poet did not belong in this country, but there I had been, strangely a part of it for a while, and to return to the Jesús María in the quiet afternoon had been to find on the border of that world, lost in the olden dreams of colonial Spain, my own enchanted Dorado. And the music of the bells on the cows walking in the silver dusk was sweet in some ridiculous way to me as that of the camel bells on any poet's golden road to Samarkand. The gentle *juajillo* whispered *peace, peace,* by the cottage doors. I had loved the Jesús María, I had loved it well, the Jesús María, and because I did, and not lightly is a poet made wise, I have hated this country ever since. Now all that I want to remember of it are the tawny pastures and shadowed groves and ruined walls tinted with rose. . . .

I don't know what happened to the Jesús María, to the Hispanic southwest. It was absorbed, it disappeared, or it turned sour. For a hundred years the vaqueros had resisted what they considered with rude insularity the sad decay of Americanization, but installment buying and gadgets and the cinema *got* them finally—and in this connection *got* is a good word—and they were to clutter the highways with second-hand Fords like white trash, these splendid hoary-handed horsemen. They listened to the radio wide-open, their sons learned English and pomaded their hair and they could not throw a *mangana,* skidding through the dust as the thousand pounds of horse hit the end of the lariat, or hold a bronc by one ear and saddle him with their free hand, but they became outcasts, schizophrenics, modern peasants produced by tractors and shiftlessness and dole and the wrong kind of advertising and pawn-shop banking and installment buying and ruinous tenant farming.

Their women have begun to act and dress like gringas,

or as the parents spitting in disgust would say, like whores—even their wives have cast the *paisano* garb for hideous store-bought clothing—the entire race has moved into ugly galvanized towns like Pena and now like the gringos these people affect to scorn any remote connection with the soil. And now they sit in these gringo towns like Indians off a reservation, having lost the last shreds of their nobility, not knowing what ails them really.

They do not know it, but they miss their village, their small *ranchitos*, that bit of land that is their *patria*, they miss the huisache shade and the quiet *laguna*, the horses galloping into water, the hunting ladinos through the brush, the crashing and the laughter of the *compañeros* and they miss their padrones. They miss the padrones, elegant, infallible, disdainful as grandees, these feudal lords who often mistreated them to the limit of forbearance, but who loved their people like children. There was something to the padrone system, after all—man does not live by bread alone, and collectively their villages were personified in the padrone. At any rate, people in that time lived more gracefully in this cruel land, and under their lords.

Now there is a venom and ugliness hanging like smog over this lost world, and I cannot adapt myself to the country or the people, I have become an alien in my own land. And with classic contention my ostrich-necked contemporaries have asked why I let this bother me, they even say that the ugly faces I see are masks of my own—*great heavens, Hindu philosophy!* But it is not so—I look around at the gringos squatting on their hunkers at the post-office instead of milking the cows, or reading the *Police Gazette* in the barbershop to put off plowing their land

—with the bilious complexions, the pin-heads and red necks and puffy faces of Rhode Island Red roosters—at this choleric, loud, cowardly, pathologically garrulous tenantry civilized by Sears Roebuck, an aura of indignation about them because they are belligerently as good as you are, rank as weed killer, salt of the earth, and I admit they oppress me. They are the kind of people to put a hand on honest weight when God isn't looking, and they are not the kind of people I was raised to believe in. . . .

So I prefer to speak of the Old Time, to remember the words, the rich raw words of another world. Perhaps I shall always be in love with the rich words of this ruined land, maybe I shall even come back to the Jesús María to die. I want to ride once more with the vaqueros, and sit around the campfire listening to old Guiterrez—old Guiterrez who was still breaking horses when he was ninety —telling his stories pared of human interest and contemptuous of hardship to the point of understatement, but rich in words. The dialect phonetic and antique, because he had learned it from his father, who was also a fierce old man and had been when he was young a *lancero* with the forces of Maximilian; he had brushed against Austrian and spahi, and the stories he told were affected with a strange color as opposed to those of Don Juan who fought *against* the French, rag-tailed and unhonored, but there had never been hard feelings between Don Juan and the elder Guiterrez, for even Don Juan admitted *qué pasa* with a shrug, that the *lanceros* were always to be found on the side that had the best horses.

That in itself had been epic, the fall of that haunted empire—Guiterrez always loved to talk of the tragic emperor, and the old horsebreaker said his father had been one of the few to escape from Querétaro after he had done his share to hold the empire, and he would look around at the young men singing in the cantina or around a campfire, and he would say, "There were men in that day, señores. What would you, señores," he would say, "whole regiments surrendered like sheep to be butchered, but not the *lanceros,* not my father, señores, *ay,* no! Not the *lanceros,* my children—they cut their way through a wall of thirty thousand men and a dozen of them lived to come to this lost world, but they never surrendered."

Guiterrez told us many other fine tales, while the eyes of the young men glittered with cruelty, or they licked their lips as they savored the gusto in a story. Only Esteban never listened, he stood in the shadows of the chuckwagon, making *panoches* for breakfast, sprinkling them with sugar like flour, and I suppose when he dies he will be making *panoches* forever in some vaquero's purgatory. The young men would sing softly, and Guiterrez would spit on the ground at their rudeness, and he would turn to me and say, "Have you ever seen the like of these *pollos,* señor? Singing and reciting, when there are stories to be told," and he would shake his huge shaggy head and speak in a voice that rumbled like Luro's—"Cortés was a poet, señor, and so was Bolívar, but they were men. And these, what has come to pass with our young men, why is it that the evil times have come on us, and we live not well?"

And for a moment I see that campfire again, the vaqueros sprawling on their saddles, smoking shuck cigarettes that smell good with the woodsmoke, the light in their faces so that a few *lavis* lines had sketched them all. There was no sound suddenly except the occasional and unutterable note of the mockingbird in a lonely *mogote,* and I remember the huisaches moved faintly, mixing the perfume of yellow blossoms in the air—I did not hear it, but I felt the gulf breeze blowing emptily through the lagoon grass, nothing else.

The campfire leapt high, greeting all the campfires in the past where stories were told by the fire. And when Guiterrez was done, I felt he was looking out in the black awful night of the lost world, and he was an exile, too. He would be silent, at last, the campfire warm and comforting against the black night of the lost world, the flame leaping high again, *greeting, greeting.* Away at the foot of the ragged mountains a coyote howled, like a lost soul. That was all, but it was enough to remember—Oh the raw rich words, the rich lost words . . .

FINIS